CHRONICLES OF OLD PARIS

EXPLORING THE HISTORIC CITY OF LIGHT

Published in the United States by:
Museyon, Inc.
20 E. 46th St., Ste. 1400
New York, NY 10017

Museyon is a registered trademark.
Visit us online at www.museyon.com

ISBN 978-0-9846334-2-5

191659

Printed in China

*I*n the film *Casablanca*, Colonel Strasser asks Humphrey Bogart's Rick, "Are you one of those people who cannot imagine the Germans in your beloved Paris." Rick replies mildly, "It's not particularly my beloved Paris."

It's a fine distinction but an important one. To me, Paris is one of those rare cities owned by everyone who lives there, or who has ever lived there. A name on a building may be that of the company which occupied it a century ago or the family who built it the century before that. In the most benign sense of the phrase, the dead walk its streets as they walked them in life. It is still the city of Marie Antoinette and Jean-Paul Sartre, of Napoleon Bonaparte and Marcel Proust, and its anthem remains Edith Piaf's defiant *"Je ne regrette rien"*— I regret nothing.

Not exclusively "my Paris," perhaps. But my Paris nonetheless.

— John Baxter

Paris, c. 1780

CHRONICLES OF OLD PARIS

TABLE OF CONTENTS

WALKING TOURS

CHAPTER 1

LOSING YOUR HEAD

THE LONG WALK OF SAINT DENIS

On the front of Notre-Dame de Paris, to the left of the main door, stands the statue of a man holding his own severed head. A halo behind his neck indicates where the head used to sit. He is Saint Denis (pronounced Der-*ny*), the patron saint of France. His expression is as relaxed as one would expect from someone who, after decapitation, walked four miles holding his head while it delivered a sermon.

Evidence of this story is understandably flimsy. A Denys or Dionysius did arrive in Lutèce or Lutetia, the site that would become Paris, around the year 250. He had been sent from Rome by Pope Fabian on a mission to convert the pagans of what was then Gaul. Rome still ruled northern Europe, and Lutèce was an important outpost. Nervous about rival belief systems, the emperor Decius was determined to stamp out Christianity in the provinces. His local representative, governor Sisinnius Fesceninus, watched uneasily as Denis installed himself on the Île de Saint-Louis, near the present site of Notre Dame, declared himself bishop and began to offer masses.

A charismatic speaker, Denis soon had a large and lively congregation, which he encouraged to smash the shrines of Rome's official gods. Local

---

< Saint Denis, carrying his own head after his decapitation, startles citizens of Roman Paris.

Saint Denis at Notre-Dame de Paris

priests demanded action from Sisinnius, who summoned Denis and his two lieutenants, Rusticus and Eleutherius, and ordered them to recant in the approved fashion: by making a sacrifice to the pagan deities. They refused, even after being elaborately tortured. Accounts claim they were scourged, racked, thrown to wild beasts and burned at the stake.

Sisinnius then ordered them beheaded before the temple to Mercury, on the highest point in the city. The soldiers charged with the task decided to save themselves the climb and kill Denis and his men at the foot of the hill, known forever after as Montmartre – the hill of the martyr. Denis, however, was as stubborn in death as in life. After the swordsman severed his head, it's said he picked it up and walked towards the summit of the hill, pausing only to wash the blood from his head at a spring. As he did so, the severed head preached a sermon on love and forgiveness. Still preaching, he strolled another four miles to the village of Catolacus. Arriving at the home of a parishioner, a wealthy woman named Catulla, he handed her his head and died at her feet. She buried him on the spot. Wheat and other plants sprouted miraculously from the grave – proof, claimed his followers, of his divine powers.

There are enough authentic details in this story to suggest it's based, however remotely, on fact. Some accounts suggest the swordsman missed his mark and sliced off only the top of his skull – by no means rare; executioners were notoriously inept. Such slipshod work may explain why he didn't die immediately, since not all such head wounds are immediately fatal. As for wheat growing on the grave, grasses and flowers often sprout from freshly dug earth as buried seeds germinate.

As Rome's influence waned and Christianity spread through the Frankish kingdom that replaced it, the former bishop became venerated throughout Christendom. His death was a popular subject for artists. Sculptors filled the vacant space above his neck with vines, signifying the plants that grew on his grave. Painters preferred to show him decapitated on the steps of a temple more lavish than anything found in a provincial backwater like Lutèce.

Basilique de Saint-Denis, 1917

By the outbreak of bubonic plague known as the Black Death in the 14th century, Saint Denis had became one of the Fourteen Holy Helpers – saints known for their influence in curing sickness. It was widely believed that a prayer to Denis would fix a headache, since he'd been beheaded. Because of his calm in the face of death, he was also credited with subduing the frenzy of rabies and even calming demonic possession.

In about 475, Saint Genevieve erected a church on the spot where Denis finally died at Catolacus. Over the next four centuries, it metamorphosed into a Gothic cathedral – Europe's first. The Cathedral Basilica of Saint Denis became the traditional site for the coronation of France's queens and the burial place of royalty – an ironic development, since the town of Saint-Denis, which grew up around the basilica, developed into a center of left-wing political activity. In modern times, it has become a bastion of the Communist Party, an important element of the "red belt" around Paris.

In Paris, Catulla built a modest shrine on the site of Denis's decapitation. Dagobert I, king of the Franks from 628 to 637, turned it into an abbey, which incorporated a Sanctum Martyrium or Martyr's Chapel. Before interring the remains of Denis and his disciples in the crypt under the Sanctum Martyrium, Dagobert placed them in miniature silver coffins. It was the start of a troubled history for the bones; some time in the 12th century, the coffins disappeared. Soon, many churches claimed to possess Denis's skull, or the top of it, a relic they believed had miraculous powers.

In 1793, the same anti-royalist revolutionaries who knocked the heads off the statues on the front of Notre Dame (convinced they were ancient kings) invaded Saint-Denis. Assuming that the crypt contained solely the remains of royalty, these rebels dragged out the bones and used the skulls as footballs, or for target practice, before dumping the skeletons into a mass grave. Today, nobody knows the whereabouts of Denis's bones – except perhaps the statue on the façade of Notre Dame. And for once, the talkative saint has nothing to say.

SEE IT: SAINT DENIS'S CITY

The Martyrdom of Saint Denis, by Léon Bonnat, c. 1880

Modern Paris preserves a number of connections to Saint Denis. On the left bank, in the Latin Quarter, behind the church of Saint-Julien-le-Pauvre, a few slabs of stone survive from the ancient Roman road. The archaeology museum under the *parvis* in front of Notre Dame shows Paris as it looked during the saint's life. The flower market behind the Conciergerie occupies the place where Denis and his followers were imprisoned and tortured.

Opposite, on the right bank, rue Saint-Denis begins in the sex shop and red light district, of which the saint would no doubt have disapproved. It ends more imposingly in the arch of the Porte de Saint-Denis. Built in 1672 by architect François Blondel and sculptor Michel Anguier to celebrate the victories of Louis XIV, the arch marks the limits of the old city.

Denis's final hours began farther west, in the 18th *arrondissement*. From Métro Notre-Dame-de-Lorette, the aptly-named rue des Martyrs climbs to rue Yvonne-Le-Tac, formerly rue Antoinette. The Métro station of Abbesses stands on the site where Denis was decapitated and a chapel at 9, rue Yvonne-le-Tac marks the spring where he paused to wash his head before continuing to the summit of Montmartre, now dominated by the domes of the Basilique du Sacré-Cœur.

How he then made his way to the village of Saint-Denis—the former Catolacus, site of the cathedral that bears his name and a distance of at least four miles—remains another of the saint's mysteries. Modern pilgrims may prefer to take the Métro to the Basilique de Saint-Denis station, saving some energy for a visit to the spectacular cathedral and its magnificently sculpted royal tombs, including those of the executed Louis XVI and his queen, Marie Antoinette.

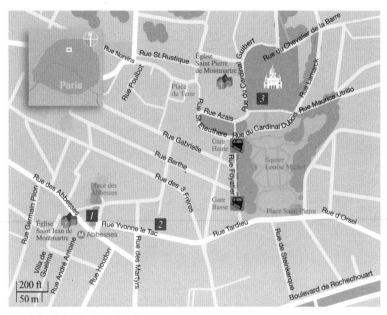

Saint Denis's Headless Walk

1 Site of Decapitation
2 Spring and Chapel
3 Summit of Mons Martins

CHAPTER 2.

LATIN LOVERS
HÉLOÏSE AND ABÉLARD

At the beginning of the High Middle Ages, Europe's brightest intellectuals were already gravitating to Paris. Most headed for the schools that clustered in the tall, narrow houses around the cathedral of Notre-Dame de Paris. The church still dominated culture and the arts, and the language of thought and learning was Latin. The district along the left bank of the Seine soon became known as the Latin Quarter.

Within this specialized world, Peter (or Pierre, or Petrus) Abélard (or Abaelardus, or Abailard) was a star. The son of a soldier from a village near Nantes, in Brittany, he turned his back on the military life and spent his teen years travelling France. He became one of the "peripatetics" – wandering students who travelled to remote monasteries, seeking out teachers, or sometimes individual books, since, in those days before printing, many classic texts existed only in a few examples, hand-copied by monks.

Around 1100, in his early twenties, Abélard came to Paris and joined the cathedral school of Notre Dame. Thin and wiry, clever and arrogant, Abélard was as sinuous as his rhetoric. His specialty was "disputation," or logic. He also wrote poetry and songs, which he performed for his classes.

Teaching in a medieval school in Paris's Latin Quarter at the time of Peter Abélard.

He launched his reputation by publicly demolishing the theories of his teacher, William of Champeaux, which earned him a number of enemies. He soon had his own school, and, despite clashes with the church authorities, who accused him of heresy, scholars came from all over Europe to hear him speak. As his classes swelled, Abélard moved uphill from the Latin Quarter to Montagne Sainte-Geneviève.

Controversy just made Abélard more attractive – even to liberal churchmen like Canon Fulbert from Brittany, who sent his ward Héloïse to Paris to study with Abélard. "Her uncle's love for her was equalled only by his desire that she should have the best education which he could possibly procure for her," Abélard wrote in his *Historia Calamitatum*.

There's some doubt about the relationship between Héloïse and Fulbert. She may have been his niece, but it's also possible she was his illegitimate daughter, which would help explain his generosity and later hostility towards Abélard.

In the many novels and films based on their story, Abélard is usually shown as a mature and dignified man in his mid-30s and Héloïse a beautiful but innocent 17. It's more likely Héloïse was about 25 and as appealing to Abélard for her intellect as for her passion and beauty. She was not only fluent in Latin, but had learned both Greek and Hebrew (neither of which Abélard spoke).

Until he met Héloïse, Abélard had avoided entanglements, but he found her irresistible. He convinced Fulbert he should move into their home as her tutor. Inevitably, the couple became lovers. "Her studies allowed us to withdraw in private, as love desired," he wrote, "and then with our books open before us, more words of love than of reading passed between us, and more kissing than teaching. My hands strayed oftener to her bosom than to the pages; love drew our eyes to look on each other more than reading kept them on our texts."

If Fulbert didn't realise what was going on, it became abundantly clear when Héloïse fell pregnant. Even then, the situation was still retrievable. Even an illegitimate child could be glossed over, particularly if the couple married quickly, or the mother gave the baby away and entered a convent in expiation of her sin.

Abélard offered to give up teaching and marry Héloïse. Fulbert was ready to cooperate, to avoid a scandal. Both men were dumbfounded when she refused. She didn't want the responsibility of depriving the world of such a great teacher as Abélard. "What penalties," she said, "would the world rightly demand of her if she should rob it of so shining a light?" Nor was she keen to become a nun and lock herself away for the rest of her life. In one of the most famous passages in the letters, she wrote: "God is my witness that if Augustus, Emperor of the whole world, thought fit to honor me with marriage and conferred all the earth on me to possess forever, it would be dearer and more honorable to me to be called not his Empress but your whore."

Running away to the home of Abelard's sister, she gave birth to a son, christened Astrolabe – the name of a scientific instrument used by sailors for navigation. This was ironic, since the relationship had now lost its way completely. In hopes of placating the family, the couple married, but agreed to keep it secret. Fulbert, however, announced it in public, to save his reputation and that of his niece. Héloïse hid from the resulting scandal in a convent, and a furious Fulbert, thinking Abélard had forced her into becoming a nun, sent men to his house, where they castrated him.

Until then, the story of Héloïse and Abélard was just another tawdry sex scandal, but this brutal attack launched their legend. While he was recuperating, Abélard's enemies, who'd been waiting their chance, attacked ferociously. The church declared him a heretic and hounded him out of Paris. Héloïse, forced to become a nun, was confined to a convent at Argenteuil. Abélard became a monk and lived in a number of monasteries—including

Saint-Denis—though none for long. In each, his contentious opinions angered colleagues, who sometimes physically attacked him. One community in the wildest part of Brittany threw him out, so he became a hermit, living in a hut of reeds chinked with mud. Even there, however, scholars sought him out, and he was eventually allowed to return to Paris and lecture.

He published *Historia Calamitatum: The Story of My Misfortunes,* an autobiography in the form of a long moan to a friend, detailing his unfortunate life. Héloïse, who had flourished as a nun and risen to become an abbess and head of her order, read it and wrote him a letter. After criticizing him for having abandoned her, she begged, "While I am denied your presence, give me at least through your words—of which you have enough and to spare—some sweet semblance of yourself."

Initially, their letters were intimate and erotic. "Even during the celebration of mass," Héloïse confessed, "when our prayers should be purer, lewd visions of those pleasures take such a hold upon my unhappy soul that my thoughts are on their wantoness instead of on our prayers." Gradually, however, the passion ebbed. What had been an outpouring of desire and emotion modified into a discussion of religious philosophy, as well as an exchange of ideas on how a convent and an order of nuns should be organized.

Nobody knows exactly how many letters they exchanged. The originals were kept at the Convent of the Paraclete, where Héloïse had become abbess, and remained there after her death in 1164. The poet Jean de Meun, author of *The Romance of the Rose,* discovered the letters in the 13th century and produced a translation that emphasised their passion but played down the less florid "Letters of Instruction." After that, the originals disappeared.

In 1974, another cache was found in Clairvaux Monastery, and a new translation restored some of the more practical language of the originals. By then, however, the world had made up its mind about Héloïse and Abélard. They became the classic illustration of love's ability to triumph over every barrier an unfeeling world can erect. As the poet Alphonse de Lamartine wrote: "One does not tell the story of Héloïse and Abelard; one sings it."

SEE IT: HÉLOÏSE AND ABÉLARD'S PARIS

According to legend, the bones of Héloïse and Abélard lie together in the cemetery of Père Lachaise. Joséphine Bonaparte, wife of Napoleon, was so touched by the story of the pair that she ordered their remains moved to the cemetery in the 19th century. A lavish Gothic stone vault marks their alleged grave. However the Oratory of the Paraclete at Nogent, where Héloïse was the abbess, claims the remains of both are still buried in its grounds and that the crypt at Père Lachaise is merely a monument.

Tomb of Héloïse and Abélard, 1815

To a surprising extent, the Latin Quarter, where Abélard once lectured, still retains some of its traditional atmosphere, although Greek restaurants are now more common than centers of scholarship. The Montagne Sainte-Geneviève, where Abélard moved his classes, is on the uphill side of the Sorbonne. The site of his school, the Abbey of Sainte-Geneviève, is occupied by the Pantheon.

For a sense of life in Paris at the time of Héloïse and Abélard, the collection of the Musée de Moyen Age de Cluny, on the corner of boulevard Saint-Germain and boulevard Saint-Michel (5th *arrondissement*) is unparalleled. Built over the ruins of Roman baths, it dates from the 1300s, when it was the palace of the Abbots of Cluny. Today, it houses one of the best collections of medieval art and artifacts in France.

For more information, visit **www.musee-moyenage.fr.**

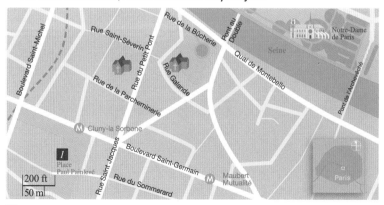

1 Musée de Moyen Age de Cluny: 6, place Paul Painlevé

Qui sait, lorsqu'le Ciel nous frappe de ses coups,
Si le plus grand'malheur n'est pas un bien pour nous?

JUSTINE,
OU
LES MALHEURS
DE LA VERTU.

O mon ami ! la prospérité du Crime est comme la
foudre, dont les feux trompeurs n'embellissent un
instant l'atmosphère, que pour précipiter dans les
abymes de la mort, le malheureux qu'ils ont ébloui.

TOME PREMIER.

EN HOLLANDE,
Chez les Libraires Associés.
1791.

CHAPTER 3.

LIBERTINE
THE DIVINE MARQUIS DE SADE

Donatien Alphonse François, Marquis de Sade was an aristocrat, revolutionary, politician, philosopher and writer, famous for his libertine sexuality and lifestyle. In a rare distinction, he was thought dangerous enough to lock up by three regimes: the Royalist, Revolutionary and Bonapartist. Despite spending a third of his life in prison, he published novels, short stories, plays, dialogues and political tracts. He is best known, however, for erotica, in particular the novels *Justine*, or *The Misfortunes of Virtue*; *Juliette*; *The 120 Days of Sodom*; and *The Philosophy of the Boudoir*. So vividly did he describe his fantasies of sexual cruelty that we still refer to such behavior by his name: sadism.

But was Sade as evil as history claims? Though he wrote extensively and with obvious pleasure about sexual torture, there is very little evidence that he ever practiced it. Courts of the time were notoriously lax about evidence, and a simple accusation was often sufficient to have a person imprisoned or even executed. Sade's worst crime was to suggest that nobles and ministers of religion were not only capable of perverted cruelty but might actively enjoy it. By those standards, scores of today's novelists, filmmakers and investigative journalists would be in cells next to him.

‹ Clockwise from top left: Marquis de Sade in Prison; illustration   21
forJustine 19 century; title page of the first edition of Justine, 1791;
L'Œuvre du marquis de Sade, edited by Guillaume Apollinaire, 1912

Portrait of the Marquis de Sade, c. 1761

Proof of Sade's lucidity lies in what he wrote on other subjects. Napoleon must have sympathized when Sade asked: "Are wars anything but the means whereby a nation is nourished, whereby it is strengthened, whereby it is buttressed?" This was exactly the philosophy that powered Bonaparte to conquer Europe.

Even modern liberals find much in Sade's work with which to agree; his belief, for instance, that "sex is as important as eating or drinking, and we ought to allow the one appetite to be satisfied with as little restraint or false modesty as the other." The New Age creed of sensible eating echoes Sade's proclamation: "Your body is the church where Nature asks to be reverenced." He also, in an unusual stance for the time, opposed capital punishment. "Until the infallibility of human judgments shall have been proved to me," he wrote, "I shall demand the abolition of the penalty of death." The marquis may have been mad, but he wasn't crazy.

Sade was born into privilege in 1740. His mother was lady-in-waiting to the Princess de Condé, wife to the Prince de Condé, financial adviser to the royal family. His Jesuit uncle had hardly completed young Donatien's education when the boy was sent off to the Seven Years' War in command of his own company of Dragoons. As a teenage colonel, Sade had plenty of opportunities, on and off the battlefield, to feed his violent sexual fantasies, though he didn't try to put them into practice until he returned to Paris at the age of 23.

In October 1763, he paid a brothel keeper two gold *louis* to deliver a 20-year-old pregnant prostitute, Jeanne Testard, to a private chapel, the walls of which he'd decorated with religious effigies and pornographic drawings. He kept her there for hours, urging her to defile the crucifixes and statues. Blasphemy was a crime regarded almost worse than murder, and once Testard swore out a complaint, Sade was arrested. His family pulled some strings to get him released, then hurriedly married him off to the daughter of a rich magistrate, too eager for the aristocratic connection to mind his new son-in-law's oddities. Sade fancied the younger of the magistrate's girls, a teenager, but had to marry the elder instead. The girl's mother, furious at seeing her children auctioned off, became Sade's lifelong enemy.

Sade moved to the family castle at Lacoste in Provence and appeared to settle down. The couple had three children and, to keep himself amused, he built a private theater and began writing plays. Behind the scenes,

Marquis de Sade in prison, 18th-century

however, he had sex with female and male servants, imported prostitutes to the castle and seduced his young sister-in-law when she came to visit.

Returning to Paris in 1778, he was soon in trouble again, accused of kidnapping and imprisoning young women, forcing them to take doses of the aphrodisiac Spanish fly. The girls were prostitutes and usually came to no harm, so the law was inclined to turn a blind eye, particularly as the offender was an aristocrat. However Sade's mother-in-law appealed to the king, who granted a *lettre de cachet,* allowing families the right to lock up troublesome relatives indefinitely without trial or appeal. Thanks to her efforts, Sade would spend most of the rest of his life in prison.

His incarceration during the Revolution may have saved his life. His wife, by then mistress of a deputy of Robespierre, was able to shuttle him from asylum to asylum, one step ahead of the guillotine. He was in the Bastille until the mob demolished it, then at the château at Picpus, where mass graves on the grounds held the decapitated corpses of fellow aristocrats. At each institution, Sade lived well. Independently rich, he could bathe daily, enjoy fresh clothes and have his favorite dishes delivered. He also wrote furiously, including short plays, which he presented with casts chosen from the inmates. Prison administrators, admiring his intellect, supplied him with writing materials. *The 120 Days of Sodom* was written on sheets intended as toilet paper and glued together in a continuous roll, making them easier to hide.

The Bastille, where Sade was imprisoned

Once the Revolution collapsed with the death of Robespierre in 1794, Sade was released and, because of his consistent championing of libertarianism in his writings, even given posts in the government. By then, however, his novels, including *Justine* and *The 120 Days of Sodom,* were in print and winning a notorious reputation. Most described how a group of supposedly moral aristocrats and pillars of the church capture young men and women, lock them in a castle, and subject them to every imaginable depravity. In each case, Sade justifies their actions: If man is indeed born with free will, he has the right to commit the worst of crimes, just as his victims have the right to avenge them.

This was too much even for Napoleon. He had Sade re-imprisoned in the asylum at Charenton. The marquis died there in 1814 in the arms of his mistress, the prison governor's 13-year-old daughter.

For a century, Sade's work was available only in highly expensive illustrated editions marketed as pornography. He was rediscovered in the early 20th century, first by the poet Guillaume Apollinaire, whose 1907 *Les Onze Mille Verges* (*The Eleven Thousand Rods*) is a tribute to Sade, and later by the Surrealists. After World War II, Jean-Paul Sartre and the Existentialists took him up. Simone de Beauvoir's *Must We Burn Sade?* suggested that the marquis merely expressed, in extreme form, many modern concepts. His books appeared in mass-market editions and achieved international fame and respect. "The Divine Marquis," as his admirers called him, was vindicated at last. Though his grave is unmarked, he wrote his own epitaph in a letter to his wife: "Either kill me or take me as I am, because I'll be damned if I ever change."

SEE IT: SADE'S FRANCE

The ruins of the Sade family castle at Lacoste, in Provence, on a rocky plateau overlooking the valley of the Vaucluse, is undoubtedly the most evocative of all sites associated with the Marquis. Nothing so spectacular remains in Paris. Sade's birthplace, the Condé palace, was demolished in the late 18th century. It once stood at 15-21, rue Condé (6th *arrondissement*).

Sade's family castle at Lacoste

When he returned to Paris in 1778, Sade lived briefly at 28, rue des Mathurins (18th) before being imprisoned at the Château de Vincennes, the Bastille, the Parc Picpus (now a cemetery) and finally the asylum at Charenton (since rebuilt and now known as Hôpital Esquirol).

He was interred on the grounds of Charenton, but the site is unknown. He asked to be buried in "an unmarked grave, allowed to grow wild, so that all trace of my resting-place should disappear from the surface of the earth, as I flatter myself that my memory will disappear from the minds of men."

CHAPTER 4

LET THEM EAT CAKE

THE MISUNDERSTOOD MARIE ANTOINETTE

Fate dealt few historical figures a stranger hand than that of Maria Antonia Josepha Johanna, Archduchess of Austria, better known as Marie Antoinette, wife of King Louis XVI, France's doomed final queen.

The second youngest of the 16 children of Emperor Francis I of Austria, Maria seemed blessed at first. Blue-eyed and blonde, she had a flair for music and dancing. She survived the smallpox that periodically swept through her family, killing or weakening other members. Had she not been so healthy, an older sister would have been chosen to prop up Austria's alliance with France following the Seven Years' War, but it was young Maria who married the future Louis XVI—a decision that led inexorably to her death on the guillotine.

From the very beginning, 14-year-old Maria and 15-year-old Louis made an odd couple. Louis was late to mature, gangling and shy, but well-read—a classic nerd. Leaving government to his ministers, he spent most of his time in the palace of Versailles, some 10 miles from Paris, indulging his love of hunting and his hobby of making locks with the palace locksmith, François Gamain. When he did go to Paris, he kept to the palaces of the Louvre or the

---

‹ *Marie Antoinette with a Rose*, by Elisabeth-Louise Vigée-Le Brun, 1783

Marie Antoinette and her family stroll the ground of the Palace of Versailles

Tuileries, sometimes taking refuge on the roof, where he couldn't hear the shouts of his angry subjects demanding bread.

Courtiers were unimpressed by their new queen's slightly protruding eyes, already burgeoning bosom and long face, typical of the Habsburg family, but assumed Louis would behave like any husband on his wedding night. The next day, they crowded into the royal apartments, expecting confirmation that the marriage had been consummated. But Marie Antoinette didn't, as was traditional, clap her hands softly to signal that the king had done his conjugal duty. In fact, he'd fallen asleep the moment they were alone, then risen early and gone hunting. After this, they slept in separate rooms.

Rumours spread that Louis had a malformed penis and feared the surgery necessary to repair it. However, the real reasons for his sexual failure were probably shyness and ignorance. Bewildered by his indifference, Marie Antoinette retired to the woods and gardens of Versailles. Influenced by Jean-Jacques Rousseau, who urged a return to a simpler life, she commanded her architect Richard Mique to build a *hameau,* or artificial village, with a farmhouse, a dairy and a mill. Dressed as shepherdesses and milkmaids, she and her ladies played at being peasants. They groomed and petted animals specially chosen for their good looks and docility, and milked cows into what looked like ordinary wooden buckets but were actually Sèvres porcelain.

Four years after she arrived in France, Marie Antoinette met the Swedish count Axel von Fersen. She felt neglected by her king, and the Count was the handsomest man at court. Both were 18. The attraction was irresistible— and mutual. The relationship continued for years, interrupted by the Count's spells in foreign capitals as a diplomat and his participation in the War of

American Independence with George Washington. The affair may have jolted Louis into looking at his wife with more interest. According to legend, one day in 1777 he walked in on her as she stepped out of the bath, and spontaneously consummated the marriage—seven years late. The first of their four children was born the following year.

Becoming a mother didn't remedy the growing unpopularity of Marie Antoinette, now referred to by the people simply as *L'Autrichienne* (The Austrian) or sometimes, because of her long neck, *L'Autruchienne* (The

Marie Antoinette, c. 1755-1770

Ostrich Woman). With increasing frequency, crowds marched from Paris to protest at the gates of Versailles, leading to one of the most enduring libels about her. When a courtier explained the mob had no bread, she supposedly responded "*Qu'ils mangent de la brioche*" ("Well, let them eat brioche").

This infamous quip was taken to mean that either she didn't care if her subjects starved, or was so out of touch that she imagined they were complaining of a lack of choice, and could have substituted the cake-like brioche for bread. Unfortunately for mythology, she never said it. Rousseau had told the story in his *Confessions,* written two years before Marie Antoinette ever saw France.

Her reputation suffered further in the Affair of the Queen's Necklace. An unscrupulous courtier, Jeanne de Saint-Rémy de Valois, used forged letters to convince her gullible admirer, the Cardinal de Rohan, that Marie Antoinette wished secretly to buy a diamond necklace ordered from the court jewelers by the former king, Louis XV, for his mistress, Madame Du Barry. The necklace was spirited away to London and never seen again. In 1786, Rohan produced the letters in court, where Louis pointed out that they were signed as no queen would ever sign: "Marie Antoinette de France." Even so, suspicions lingered that she was involved.

Marie Antoinette led to the scaffold, pen and ink drawings by David, 1793

Marie Antoinette at the guillotine, October 16, 1793

As revolution loomed, Louis responded clumsily. Count von Fersen's plan to whisk the family and members of the court over the border failed when the king dithered about who should go. Those fleeing the palace were captured and returned to Paris within the week. In May 1792, a mob broke into the Tuileries Palace. They put the king on trial in November. Among those who testified against Louis was François Gamain, the locksmith, who revealed the secret of an iron chest they had made together to hide important papers. In January 1793, the fallen King of France was beheaded in the Place de la Révolution, now the Place de la Concorde.

Marie Antoinette and her children were imprisoned until October, when she was charged with sending millions to her family in Austria, arranging assassinations and holding orgies at Versailles. The worst charge of all came from her 10-year-old son, Louis-Charles, who was coerced into accusing his mother of incest. In her final letter to her sister, Marie Antoinette begged her to forgive the boy: "Remember his youth and how easy it is to speak to a child, yet how hard it is for him to understand you."

Marie Antoinette was executed on October 16, 1793. On her way to the execution block, she was paraded through Paris with her hair cropped and her hands tied behind her back. She wore a plain cotton dress and a red cap, a symbol of the Revolution. Just before her death, she said with resignation: "I have seen all, I have heard all, I have forgotten all." She was only 37.

SEE IT: MARIE ANTOINETTE'S FRANCE

Most sites associated with Marie Antoinette are located outside Paris. These include the former royal park at Rambouillet and Compiègne, where she was received on her arrival from Austria. At Versailles, the *hameau* still stands, while the palace contains numerous reminders of her reign.

In Paris, the Musée Carnavalet (23, rue de Sévigné, 3rd *arrondissement*) devotes a room to the former queen, including many paintings and some of her possessions. Her chocolate-makers, Debauve & Gallais, remain in business in the original shop (30, rue des Saints-Pères, 7th). They still sell the chocolate discs, called *pistoles*, flavored with almond oil, coffee, vanilla and orange, that they developed for her to make medicine more palatable.

The Conciergerie (Île de la Cité, 1st), where the queen and her children were imprisoned after Louis's death, was rebuilt in the middle of the 19th century. Today it holds a museum to all victims of The Terror, including the queen, whose cell is recreated.

Louis and Marie Antoinette were initially buried in the Madeleine Cemetery. After the transfer of their remains to the Basilica of Saint-Denis, a Chapelle Expiatoire or Chapel of Expiation was built on the site (Square Louis XVI, 8th). Inside, larger-than-life-size statues show the king and queen in ecstatic poses, embracing religion and being assumed into heaven.

An unusual memento from the queen's reign remains at 17, rue Montorgeuil (1st). There stands a door with a lintel engraved Passage de la Reine de Hongrie (Passage of the Queen of Hungary). Legend has it the passage takes its name from Julie Bécheur, a shopkeeper at the nearby Les Halles market, who was delegated to present a petition to the queen. When Marie Antoinette met Bécheur, she remarked that the vegetable-seller resembled her mother, the Queen of Hungary. The story quickly spread, and to commemorate it, locals renamed the passage where Bécheur lived.

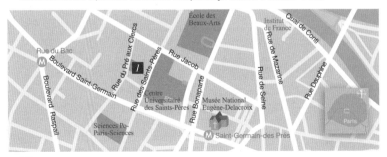

1 Debauve & Gallais: 30, rue des Saints-Pères

CHAPTER 5

"LIKE A BREATH ON THE BACK OF YOUR NECK"

THE USEFUL INVENTION OF DR. GUILLOTIN

In 1770, as Marie Antoinette was paraded through Paris on her way to marry the future Louis XVI, the 14-year-old Archduchess of Austria's coach was stopped outside a Jesuit school by some schoolboys. Twelve-year-old Maximilien Robespierre read a speech of welcome he'd written himself. Some 23 years later, he signed her death warrant as one of the leaders of the Revolution, just as he had signed the death warrant of the king and almost every aristocrat in France. The following year, he too was executed.

All of them died on a machine that the French Revolution made notorious—the guillotine. Yet Dr. Joseph-Ignace Guillotin, the man who perfected the contraption was a staunch opponent of capital punishment. He hoped his creation would make executions less common; even end them altogether.

Traditionally, execution, at least of common criminals, was a public spectacle. Felons usually hanged and religious heretics were burned alive. In France, breaking on the wheel was common—the victim tied to a wagon wheel and his bones broken one by one with an iron bar. Unless the victim or his relatives paid to have the first blow be a fatal one, the condemned person could remain on display and in agony for a day or more. Even by the

Traditionally, executions by guillotine took place in public and at dawn.

standards of the time this was considered barbaric; in 1791 Louis XVI made it illegal.

Since ancient times, aristocrats had been despatched more quickly and privately: strangled, stabbed or poisoned. In 1477, the Duke of Clarence asked to be drowned in a barrel of his favorite drink, the sweet wine called Malmsey. In 1327, England's King Edward II, rumored to be homosexual, was stabbed through his rectum with a red-hot poker, so as to leave no mark. Even into the 20th century, members of the British House of Lords convicted of a capital crime could request a noose of slippery silk instead of the more abrasive hemp.

All that changed with the French Revolution of 1789. Since the motto of the Revolutionaries was *Liberte, egalite, fraternite* (Liberty, Equality, Brotherhood) the newly elected Chamber of Deputies argued that these rules should also cover executions. It was welcomed news to Dr. Guillotin, one of the deputies, to whom the sight of prisoners tortured in public had always been distasteful. He was convinced that if one removed the element of spectacle from execution, people would lose interest and imprisonment would replace death as a punishment.

On October 10, 1789, Guillotin proposed that all executions henceforth take place in private. Only one method should be used, and it must be humane. The Assembly agreed and on March 25, 1791, voted for beheading.

But who was to carry out such a sentence? The axe and the sword were notoriously inefficient, as were the men who wielded them.

Guillotin then suggested a system already used in Italy and parts of Britain. The condemned person was placed face down on a scaffold, and a heavy blade dropped on his neck. If the blade was sharp and the weight sufficient, it severed the head with one blow and the victim supposedly felt nothing. Guillotin was so enthusiastic that he spoke as if he'd already developed such a device. "With my machine," he announced, "at worst, the patient will feel no more than a breath on the back of his neck!" The deputies laughed, but endorsed the plan anyway.

Having sold them on "his" mechanism, Guillotin had to produce a working version. He recruited a surgeon, Antoine Louis, who had already experimented with the device. They hired Tobias Schmidt, a German harpsichord-maker, to build it. As a professional courtesy, they consulted Charles-Henri Sanson, the official executioner. Sanson welcomed the idea; decapitating by hand was hard work. Poor lighting often made him miss the neck entirely. Besides, he was usually given mediocre swords, which broke.

Together, Louis, Guillotin and Schmidt designed a scaffold consisting of two wooden uprights, joined by a beam across the top. Between the uprights, a wooden block slid in grooves greased with tallow. Set into the lower face of the block was the fatal steel blade. As the victim knelt between the uprights, a rope released the block, which dropped swiftly, severing the head.

The technical problems were considerable. Which form of blade was better: a straight edge, a diagonal or a crescent? What was the ideal weight of the block? Schmidt's workshop was on the Cour du Commerce, an alley that ran behind the Procope, France's first café and a favorite meeting place for intellectuals. The café's patrons protested at the blood that ran down the gutters whenever Schmidt and Guillotin tried their latest prototype on sheep. In honor of the sacrificed animals, the block holding the blade is still called by the French word for sheep: a *mouton*.

The first prototype was installed in the Place de la Révolution, today the Place de la Concorde. It stood on a platform with 24 steps, raising it well above the crowd so that all could see. Since raw wood would show blood, everything was painted red. The machine was used for the first time on April 25, 1792, to execute a thief named Nicolas-Jacques Pelletier. His head fell cleanly at the first stroke. After that, more of the devices were set up in other public places around Paris, and others shipped to all the cities of France.

A British versifier, unable to find a rhyme for Guillotin (pronounced Ghee-oh-*tan*), changed it to "Ghee-oh-*teen,* " calling the doctor "The patriot keen/Guillotine." Since, in French, the addition of the letter "e" to a name normally indicates femininity, the machine immediately became *Madame La Guillotine*.

In order to create a classless society, the Revolutionaries decreed that every aristocrat must die, as well as any priest, monk or nun who wouldn't renounce the Catholic Church. Then the Revolutionaries turned on each other, sending to the scaffold all who opposed the latest changes in policy.

One by one, those who had led the uprising became its victims. So many were condemned that Sanson, the public executioner, even with the aid of his two sons and six assistants, barely managed to keep up. Between 1792 and 1795, he personally beheaded 2,794 people, sometimes at the rate of one a minute. Before the slaughter ended in 1794, between 18,000 and 40,000 people had felt Dr. Guillotin's "breath on the neck." One of the last was Robespierre.

Dr. Guillotin, a loyal servant of the Revolution, survived The Terror only to die of an infected boil in 1814. By then, he'd given up begging the government to call the machine something else, and changed the family name instead.

The guillotine remained the official method of execution in France until the abolition of capital punishment in 1981.

SEE IT: REVOLUTIONARY PARIS

Home of Tobias Schmidt

A brass plate in front of the Hôtel de Crillon, on the Place de la Concorde, marks where the first guillotine once stood. The house of Tobias Schmidt, who made a fortune producing the machine, still exists at 6, Cour du Commerce (6th *arrondissement*), marked by a barely legible plaque.

Almost diagonally opposite at No. 8 is the print shop of Jean-Paul Marat, a radical pamphleteer who advocated even more executions—as many as 270,000. Marat escaped the guillotine, only to be stabbed in his bath at 18, rue de l'École de Medicine (6th). Nearby, on boulevard Saint-Germain, a statue marks the former house of Georges Danton, another leader of the Revolution. Executed on Robespierre's orders, he told Sanson, the executioner, "Don't forget to hold up my head to the people. It's well worth seeing."

Many of the victims of The Terror are buried in mass graves at Picpus Cemetery (12th). The 1,300 interred there include nobles, priests, monks, military men, commoners and 197 women, including 51 aristocrats and 23 nuns.

1 Home of Tobias Schmidt: 6, Cour du Commerce
2 Print Shop of Jean-Paul Marat: 8, Cour du Commerce
3 Home of Jean-Paul Marat: 18, rue de l'École de Medicine

CHAPTER 6

THE GENERAL AND HIS LADY

NAPOLEON BONAPARTE AND JOSÉPHINE

For sheer grandeur, few paintings in the Louvre equal Jacques-Louis David's *The Coronation of Napoleon*. Ten meters wide by six meters tall, it shows the moment in 1804 when, about to be crowned by a representative of the Pope, Napoleon took the crown and placed it on his own head to show he was above all other powers, even the mighty church. Then he took another crown and ennobled the woman kneeling at his feet—his wife Joséphine.

David's work delighted the emperor. "What relief, what truthfulness!" he said. "This is not a painting; one walks in this picture." One of Napoleon's most enthusiastic admirers, David knew he had created his masterwork. "I shall slide into posterity in the shadow of my hero," the painter said with satisfaction.

Napoleon Bonaparte is the one Frenchman everybody recognizes. Short, plump, pale, wearing a cocked hat, right hand thrust inside the vest of his uniform, he's as distinctive a figure as Adolf Hitler—whose career, in many ways, Bonaparte foreshadowed. His wife, Joséphine, is more obscure, yet her influence on her husband's career is crucial. In a world he was determined to impose his will upon, she was an elusive and wayward element, constantly reminding him that he was, after all, only human.

The times created Napoleon. While the Revolution of 1789 destroyed the centuries-old feudal system of France, it left a power vacuum. As interim governments dithered, Bonaparte, then a minor military commander, seized his opportunity. In 1795, as a 26-year-old brigadier general, he routed a Royalist mob on the streets of Paris with cannon loaded not with explosive shells but smaller balls of metal; the rioters fled, he boasted, after just "a whiff of grape-shot."

Napoleon as 1st Consul, Jean Auguste Dominique Ingres, 1803-4

Promoted to commander of the French army in Italy, he learned that taking charge came naturally to him. "I love power," he said. "But it is as an artist that I love it. I love it as a musician loves his violin, to draw out its sounds and chords and harmonies." Driven by his motto, "Audacity! Always audacity," he mobilized France and went to war with the world, determined to create an empire all his own. Within 20 years, he controlled Europe from Spain to Sweden, and was eyeing India, North Africa and Russia. Only Britain held out, thanks to its superior Navy and the genius of Admiral Horatio Nelson. In 1804, a grateful France crowned Napoleon emperor.

Few great soldiers have also been gifted administrators with a clear vision of history. Napoleon possessed all three qualities. But this most famous of Frenchmen was not, strictly speaking, French. Corsica, the Mediterranean island where he was born, was officially part of France but culturally closer to Italy, from where his ancestors, the Buonapartes, had come.

Being an outsider helped him. He had fewer of the old loyalties that might have held back his ambition. All the same, he demanded absolute dedication from his own staff. When someone recommended a new officer as "a patriot," he demanded, "But is he a patriot for me?" Shrewdly, he rotated officers in and out of favor. The favorite of one week could be coldly dismissed the next, only to be restored again—a method that kept everyone eager to please. Faithful helpers were well rewarded. Each time he conquered a new country, he installed a relative or one of his marshals as king.

The Revolution had tried and failed to remake the whole of French society, aiming to abolish the aristocracy and the church, issue a unified set of laws and create a free and equal system of education. Attempts were made to reorganize the system of weights and measures and to rationalize the calendar

Emperor Napoleon Bonaparte

by renaming the months. Napoleon took the best of these ideas and used his genius for organization to put them into practice.

The *Code Napoleon*, unveiled in 1807, swept away local and ancient legal customs and precedents, replacing them with a system that survives to this day.

He imposed a single tax system, eradicating "tax farming," under which individual aristocrats taxed people in their areas and kept a share for themselves. He established the metric system of measuring weight and distance; miles became kilometers, kilograms replaced pounds and liters supplanted pints. To the horror of the church, he also instituted civil divorce and decriminalized homosexuality. In 1810, to a stunned audience of priests, he announced, "I am a monarch of God's creation, and you reptiles of the earth dare not oppose me. I render an account of my government to none save God and Jesus Christ."

As his armies swept across Europe, toppling ancient and corrupt monarchies, Napoleon seemed the very spirit of the modern age. Artists, writers and composers were inspired. British poet William Wordsworth wrote of the Revolution: "Bliss was it in that dawn to be alive, but to be young was

Portrait of the Empress Joséphine, Queen of Italy, by Andrea Appiani, 1807

very heaven!" In the same spirit, Beethoven named his Third Symphony "The Buonaparte," and Jacques-Louis David painted Napoleon on a rearing horse, long hair flowing, as he led his troops across the Alps to plunge into Italy and unite its squabbling kingdoms under French control.

For all his liberalizing and innovation, Napoleon remained a tyrant, responsible to nobody. His secret police force was extensive and ruthless, and any dissent in the countries he occupied was brutally suppressed. Thomas Jefferson condemned him. "What year of his military life has not consigned a million of human beings to death, to poverty and wretchedness?" Jefferson demanded. "What field in Europe may not raise a monument of the murders, the burnings, the desolations, the famines and miseries it has witnessed from him?"

The love of Napoleon's life was Marie Josèphe Rose Tascher de La Pagerie, whom he always called Joséphine. Six years older, she became his lover in 1795 and they married a year later. His enemies sneered at his choice. She was another foreigner—born on the Caribbean island of Martinique— and her first husband, Alexandre de Beauharnais, had been guillotined in the Revolution, not entirely for his aristocracy, but for his incompetence in defending the city of Mainz against the Prussians. With two children and an extravagant lifestyle to support, Joséphine became the mistress of various powerful men, the last of whom, Paul François Jean Nicolas, Vicomte de Barras, encouraged a liaison with the young Napoleon to get her off his hands.

Joséphine had a reputation for sensuality. A British cartoon shows her and another woman dancing naked before a drunken Barras, though this may simply have been a reaction by prudish Britain to France's revealing fashions. For a woman so sophisticated, the naïve young general was an easy target, particularly since she accommodated his sexual quirks, including a taste for women with pungent body odors. He supposedly wrote her from

James Gillray's 1805 caricature, *Paul Barras being entertained by the naked dancing of two wives of prominent men, Tallien and Bonaparte.*

the battlefield, "*Je reviens en trois jours, ne te laves pas.*" ("I will return in three days. Don't wash.") She also ignored his odd table manners. Arguing that all food ended up in the same place, he'd start with dessert, take some soup, and only then get to the meat course.

In return, he indulged her spendthrift habits, although he was furious when, during his absence on an expedition to Egypt between 1798 and 1800, she bought the château of Malmaison on the outskirts of Paris and spent a fortune on restoration. She defied him and kept spending, creating lavish gardens with one of the world's greatest collections of roses, her special love. Later, she added a heated orangery to grow pineapples and populated the grounds with ostriches, llamas, a seal, an emu and some kangaroos.

Joséphine's passion for collecting mirrored some of Napoleon's own preoccupations. He celebrated scholarship, creating academies that honored scientists and intellectuals just as the old regime had deferred to hereditary aristocrats. When he invaded Egypt, he took 167 mathematicians, geographers and artists with him. While his forces routed the feeble Egyptian army and attempted, unsuccessfully, to defeat Nelson and the British Navy, these *savants* documented and analyzed the remains of an ancient culture. Among their discoveries was the Rosetta Stone, which made it possible for the first time to decipher Egyptian hieroglyphs. Their report, *Description de l'Égypte*, published between 1809 and 1829, ran to 30 volumes, half of them devoted to vivid paintings and engravings that inflamed European artists with new ideas in architecture and design.

Madame Récamier, by Jacques-Louis David, 1800

The concept of France as an imperial power ignited the national imagination. Statues and paintings of Napoleon showed him crowned with the traditional Roman wreath of laurel and wearing robes that would not have looked out of place on Julius Caesar. New buildings borrowed ideas from Roman and Greek architecture. Napoleon's favorite architects, Charles Percier and Pierre Fontaine, built the Roman-style Arc de Triomphe du Carrousel in the Tuileries Gardens and renovated the Palace of the Tuileries (now destroyed), replacing elaborate décor with classical simplicity. This fashion extended to clothing. People no longer wore powdered wigs, varnished leather boots or tight jackets with high starched collars. Clothing for women became loose and flowing, a style made instantly fashionable in 1800 when David painted the leading Parisian hostess, Juliette Récamier, dressed in antique style, lounging on a Roman-style couch and displaying—shockingly—bare feet.

Once Napoleon became emperor, many of his earliest supporters turned on him, particularly the artists. During the anarchist uprising of the Commune in 1871, the Communards burned down the Palace of the Tuileries as a symbol of the hated imperial rule. When Beethoven learned of Napoleon's coronation, he raged, "So he is no more than a common mortal! Now, too, he will tread underfoot all the rights of man, indulge only his ambition; now he will think himself superior to all men, become a tyrant!" He ripped off the cover page of his manuscript of the Third Symphony, with its dedication to Napoleon, and would have destroyed the whole score if friends had not prevented him. After that, it was known as the *Eroica*, Italian for the "heroic."

If Napoleon's relationship with his admirers was stormy, that with Joséphine was worse. At the end of his life, he confided to a friend, "I truly loved my

Joséphine, but I did not respect her."
Both had affairs, particularly after it
became evident that Joséphine could
not produce the son and heir needed to
carry on the empire. In 1810, Napoleon
divorced her. She retired to Malmaison
and died four years later of pneumonia,
which she caught while taking Tsar
Alexander of Russia on a tour of
her gardens.

To replace her, Napoleon married
Princess Marie Louise of Austria.
He was too busy to actually attend
in person, so the wedding took place

Marie-Louise, by François Gérard

by proxy. When they finally got together, she did give him a son in 1811.
Christened Napoleon François Joseph Charles, he was known from birth as
the King of Rome but popularly called *L'Aiglon*, the young eagle. Always
sickly, he caught tuberculosis, and although crowned Napoleon II in 1814,
reigned for only two weeks before dying at age 21. He had no children.

Militarily, Napoleon met his match when he invaded Russia in 1812. His
Grande Armée reached Moscow, only to find that the retreating Russians
had torched it to deny him food and shelter. His retreat back to France in
the depths of the Russian winter was his greatest defeat. He was forced to
abdicate in 1813 and surrendered to the British, who imprisoned him on
Elba, an island off the Italian coast. They underestimated his cunning. A year
later, he escaped and, in a mere 100 days, rallied his old army, took on the

Napoleon's return from the Island
of Elba, March 7, 1815

The Battle of Waterloo. June 18, 1815,
by Clément-Auguste Andrieux, 1852

Death of Napoleon at St. Helena, May 5, 1821, Charles de Steuben, c. 1828

Arrival of la Dorade at Courbevoie on 14 December 1840, Henri-Félix-Emmanuel Philippoteaux, 1867

combined forces of Russia, Prussia, Austria, Sweden and Britain near the Belgian town of Waterloo, and came close to crushing them all. After his defeat, the British commander, the Duke of Wellington, admitted privately that the battle was "a damned close-run thing."

Having let Bonaparte escape once, the British were not about to repeat the mistake. They imprisoned him on St. Helena, a speck of an island in the South Atlantic, one of the remotest places on earth. He survived for only six years, a forlorn figure, increasingly ill. Though rumors surrounded his death, with suggestions that he had been poisoned by arsenic, he probably died of a gastric ulcer. His last words were, "*France, armée, tête d'armée, Joséphine.*"("France, army, head of the army, Joséphine.") In his will, he asked to be buried on the banks of the Seine, but the British, nervous about another uprising, interred him on St. Helena. Since nobody could agree whether the tombstone should read "Napoleon Bonaparte" or just, in the style of royalty, "Napoleon," it was left blank.

Napoleon's remains stayed in exile until 1840, when it was finally deemed safe to bring them to France. They arrived on the frigate *Belle-Poule*, which was painted entirely black. After a state funeral, he was installed in a massive sarcophagus of red porphyry, in the crypt of the Hôtel des Invalides, the museum to the army of France, his first and only true love, and one that remained faithful to him to the end.

NAPOLEON'S PARIS

The hearse of Napoleon under the Arc de Triomphe de l'Étoile

"Greatness is nothing unless it be lasting," Napoleon said. In that case, Paris is his best monument, with numerous buildings reflecting Greek and Roman architecture. The Arc de Triomphe, built to commemorate his victories, dominates the right bank at the top of the Champs-Élysées and offers a panoramic view of the city. The columns at the center of Place Vendôme and Place du Châtelet also celebrate his triumphs in Roman style, as do the Fontaine de Mars on rue Saint-Dominique, the Fontaine de la Paix on rue Bonaparte and the Fontaine de Médicis, next to the Luxembourg Gardens. His old military school, the École Militaire, still stands at the head of the Champ de Mars.

Portrait of Empress Joséphine, 1805

The Louvre contains numerous trophies and artworks collected on his campaigns as well as reconstructions of his private apartments. It is also counts among its collections Pierre-Paul Proud'hon's 1805 portrait of Joséphine and David's enormous picture of Napoleon's coronation at Notre Dame, as well as the famous portrait of a barefoot Madame Récamier.

However, one gets a more immediate sense of Napoleon from the Musée de l'Armée in the Invalides, which contains personal memorabilia and uniforms, in addition to Ingres's portrait of Napoleon as emperor, self-consciously posed to resemble Julius Caesar. It is also home to the emperor's impressive tomb.

For a view of Napoleon's private world, the home Joséphine purchased at Malmaison has been lovingly restored and remains the one indispensible stop for anyone interested in their life together.

Malmaison, 1807

For a fragrant reminder of the romance of Napoleon and Joséphine, the Worth perfume Je Reviens is named in memory of Napoleon's letter to Joséphine urging her not to wash.

CHAPTER 7.

PASSION'S PLAYTHINGS
GEORGE SAND AND FRÉDÉRIC CHOPIN

After the fall of Napoleon in 1815, a wave of Romanticism swept through the arts in Europe. New visionaries looked beyond the classicism of the Age of Reason: Beethoven in music, Byron in poetry, the Brontës in prose and Delacroix in painting. Artists were free to express extravagant emotions, live unconventionally and embrace the most extreme views.

Nobody did so more proudly than Amantine Aurore Lucile Dupin, Baroness Dudevant. The daughter of an army lieutenant, she was born in the home of a fellow officer where her parents had gone to a dance. "She will be lucky," said her aunt, "for she was born among the roses and to the sound of music." At 19, she married Baron Casimir Dudevant and had two children by him, but by 1831 she abandoned the marriage to embark on a "romantic rebellion."

Moving to Paris, she became a hack journalist—a "newspaper mechanic," as she described it—for the daily *Le Figaro*. At night, she prowled the cafés of the Latin Quarter, ears tuned to new gossip. No respectable woman went to such places, so she began dressing as a man and behaving like one, demanding to be addressed as *"mon frère"* (my brother) and smoking cigars,

a habit picked up from her friend Marie d'Agoult, lover of composer Franz Liszt. When her first novel, *Indiana,* was published in 1832, she adopted a male name too: George Sand.

Delacroix's 1838 portrait of Sand and Chopin was cut into two

Though she had affairs with women, Sand preferred men, ideally young, weak and gifted. Alfred de Musset fit the bill perfectly. Six years her junior, pale, chronically ill and usually dressed in pink, he made an odd suitor. But his passionate poetry moved her. In 1833, with her children in tow, she and Musset traveled to Venice, the place regarded as the wellspring of the Romantic movement by Northern Europeans. As a romantic gesture, it fell flat. Musset got sick and Sand fell in love with his doctor, Pietro Pagello.

Musset returned to France alone, and, seething with passion and spite, wrote *Gamiani*, or *Two Nights of Excess,* a pornographic novella about Countess Gamiani, Paris's most flamboyant hostess, who enjoys sex with men, women and animals. It had just been published, anonymously, when Sand arrived in Paris with Pagello. Shortly after, she and Musset took up where they had left off, while the doctor returned to Venice, disconsolate. After five months, Sand tired of the sickly Musset as well. She cut off her hair and sent it to him as a gesture of renunciation, and fled to her family chateau in Nohant, south of the Loire.

When she met the Polish composer and pianist Frédéric Chopin at the home of his lover Marie d'Agoult in 1836, she was ready for another affair. He wasn't as impressed with her. "What a repulsive woman Sand is!" he wrote to a friend. "But is she really a woman? I am inclined to doubt it." By June 1838, however, they were a couple. Once again, Sand decided the situation called for a romantic idyll in the south and whisked Chopin to Majorca.

But the island's cold, wet weather aggravated Chopin's tuberculosis. "I have been sick as a dog during these past two weeks," he wrote. "Three doctors have visited me. The first said I was going to die; the second said I was breathing my last; and the third said I was already dead." It took weeks for his

The house of George Sand in Nohant, 1955

piano to arrive from Paris. When it did, he composed furiously, while Sand re-wrote her 1833 novel *Lélia*. She didn't doubt she had found the love of her life. "This Chopin is an angel," she told d'Agoult. "His kindness, his tenderness and his patience worry me sometimes. I think that he is too fine, too exquisite and too perfect to live a long time of our gross and heavy terrestrial life."

In Paris, Sand introduced Chopin to her friends, including the painter Eugène Delacroix. Though Delacroix is best known as a master of the crowded canvases of historical scenes typical of the Romantic movement, he painted an intimate double portrait of Chopin at the piano and Sand doing needlework. This domesticity became the pattern of their lives for the nine years they spent together. They didn't repeat the experiment of Majorca and instead spent their summers in Nohant from 1839 to 1846. Some evenings, they presented plays in the small private theaters on the estate. On others, Chopin accompanied the singer Pauline Viardot on ballads from the time of Sand's grandmother. Liszt visited, as did Delacroix, who wrote "when we are not together to dine, eat lunch, play billiards or to walk, we read in our room or doze on the settee. From time to time, a thread of music from Chopin weaves itself into the song of the nightingales and the odor with the rose trees."

Such tranquility couldn't last. The Romantic movement was overtaken by a new spirit of experimentation. Sand became increasingly political and impatient with Chopin's poor health. She expressed her frustration in the novel *Lucrezia Floriani*, about an Eastern European prince and a middle-aged actress who sacrifices herself to care for him. In 1846, when Chopin

A cast of Chopin's left hand

sided with Sand's daughter Solange in a family dispute over money, the break became final.

Penniless and in increasingly poor health, Chopin continued to perform. In September 1849, after a tour of Britain, he returned to Paris and collapsed. He died in October, at only 39. Solange was at his bedside and her husband, the sculptor Auguste Clésinger, made a death mask and a cast of his left hand. Sand didn't visit her former lover in his last days, nor was she among the 3,000 people at his funeral.

Sand lived for another 37 years. Ever more political, she started her own newspaper and campaigned for women's rights. In June 1848, the working class of Paris revolted against the failure of the government to introduce more liberal policies. The uprising was a bloody fiasco and ushered in the even more repressive regime of Louis Napoleon, later called Emperor Napoleon III.

Disappointed, Sand retired to Nohant and concentrated on novels and plays. But something of the old spirit remained. "Once my heart was captured," she wrote nostalgically, "reason was shown the door, deliberately and with a sort of frantic joy. I accepted everything, I believed everything, without struggle, without suffering, without regret, without false shame. How can one blush for what one adores?"

SEE IT: SAND'S PARIS

A plaque at 31, rue de Seine (6th *arrondissement*) marks the house where George Sand stayed when she came to Paris in 1831. Shortly after, she moved into the boarding house of her lover Jules Sandeau at 21, quai des Grands Augustins, also in the 6th. They often ate at what was then the modest Restaurant Lapérouse (51, quai des Grands Augustins), which retains the sumptuous decoration and discreet private rooms from its earlier incarnation as a brothel. In the top apartment at 19, quai Malaquais, she pursued her affairs with Alfred de Musset and Pietro Pagello.

For most of their life together, Sand and Frédéric Chopin lived in the 9th *arrondissement*. At 16, rue Pigalle (now No. 20), they rented separate apartments in the same building—one where Chopin could work, the other for Sand and her children. In 1842, they moved to the Square d'Orléans (entered, weekdays only, through 80, rue Taitbout). Their studios were at opposite corners—Sand's above the coach house at No. 5 and Chopin's on the ground floor at No. 9. In the evenings, they entertained in the apartment of a friend at No. 7. The most enduring and detailed memorial to their time in Paris is the former home of painter Ary Scheffer at 16, rue Chaptal, now the Musée de la Vie Romantique. The ground floor is devoted entirely to Sand, including a reconstruction of the salon at Nohant, together with letters, portraits and memorabilia. The château at Nohant is also preserved as a museum and the site of her grave.

The Musée Eugène Delacroix (6, rue de Furstenberg, 6th) contains paintings done during the artist's visits to Sand and Chopin at Nohant. Delacroix's joint portrait of Sand and Chopin has since been cut in two. The Chopin portion is in the Louvre and the Sand part in Copenhagen's Ordrupgaard Museum. Chopin died at 12, place Vendôme (1st) and is buried in Père Lachaise Cemetery, in a grave topped by a statue by Auguste Clésinger.

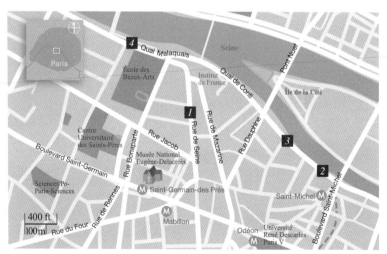

George Sand's Left Bank

1 Home of George Sand: 31, rue de Seine
2 Home of Jules Sandeau: 21, quai des Grands Augustins
3 Restaurant Lapérouse: 51, quai des Grands Augustins
4 Home of Pietro Pagello: 19, quai Malaquais

CHAPTER 8.

A NOVEL IN STONE
NOTRE DAME AND HER GUARDIAN

Next to the Eiffel Tower, no building in Paris is more instantly recognizable than the cathedral of Notre-Dame de Paris. Like a giant ocean liner in stone, it dominates the Île de la Cité, one of the two islands that divide the Seine. Its bells, deeper in tone than those of any other Parisian church, toll out with a measured boom to signify events of national significance; the feasts of the church year, or the death of some great figure of politics or art.

It was not always this way. As recently as 200 years ago, Notre Dame was close to ruin, its foundations waterlogged, its stonework rotting. France too was in crisis. A new emperor, Louis-Philippe, had just been crowned, launching what some called a "finance aristocracy." The egalitarian spirit of the 1789 Revolution was a distant memory. Nobody cared about the neglected patrimony of France, least of all its great churches. The new culture had only one god – money. "From now on," said millionaire businessman Jacques Lafitte with great content, "bankers will rule."

Much of the credit for saving Notre Dame goes to a young writer. In 1830, Victor Hugo was only 29. His father, an army officer, hated both the church and the monarchy. Hugo's mother, on the other hand, was Catholic and a

‹ Lon Chaney in *The Notre Dame de Paris*, 1923

55

Victor Hugo, 1829

royalist. Tired of trailing after her husband to military bases all over Europe, she brought Victor and his three brothers to Paris. He grew up a passionate supporter of the Bourbon kings and a deep admirer of *le patrimoine* – the traditions and cultural treasures of France, including the Cathedral of Notre Dame.

For the young Hugo, buildings assumed a mystical significance. In a still largely illiterate society, they were history written without words. "There exists in this era," he wrote, "for thoughts written in stone, a privilege absolutely comparable to our current freedom of the press. It is the freedom of architecture." Although he'd published only one short novel, he persuaded his publisher Gosselin to commission an historical epic, set during the Middle Ages, when life in Paris was as much in turmoil as it was in Hugo's own time. Its focus would be the Cathedralé Notre-Dame de Paris.

Biting off more than one can chew is a common fault of young writers, and Hugo became ambition's victim. France was changing so radically that each day brought another plot idea. By September 1830, Gosselin had lost patience. If the book wasn't finished in six months, he announced, the deal was off. Hugo set to work. He bought quantities of paper, a large bottle of ink and a heavy woollen cloak: once he began writing, he couldn't stop to replenish the fire. He also dismissed the servants and locked himself in. For the next six months, he went out only to pay nocturnal visits to Notre Dame and prowl every dank, crumbling corner.

To Hugo, Notre Dame became an open book, to be read as easily as any medieval text. "When a man understands the art of seeing," he wrote, "he can trace the spirit of an age and the features of a king even in the knocker on a door." All he needed was a hero. From workmen, he heard stories of a handicapped stonemason named Trajan, who suffered from the spinal distortion known as *kyphosis,* commonly called a "hunch" or "hump" back. Though Trajan avoided his fellow workers, they always addressed him respectfully as "*M. le Bossu*" – "Mr. Hunchback."

Scene of *The Hunchback of Notre-Dame*, c. 1860s

Trajan was the spark that ignited *Notre-Dame de Paris,* better known as *The Hunchback of Notre-Dame*. Hugo set the story in 1482, when the cathedral was halfway through its second century, but already showing its age. As the people of Paris surged through the *parvis*, or open space in front of the church, nobody noticed a figure looking down on them – "a strange spectator, with a neck so strained, a visage so hideous that, in his motley accoutrement of red and violet, he might have been taken for one of those stone monsters through whose mouths the long gutters of the cathedral have discharged their waters for six hundred years."

The man is Quasimodo, the bell-ringer. Not only does he suffer from *kyphosis*, a growth covers one eye, distorting his face, and he's deaf from the constant tolling of the bells. His handicaps only make him more sensitive to beauty, and when he sees a lovely gypsy girl, Esmerelda, about to be hanged as a witch, compassion drives him to intervene.

"He was seen to glide down the façade," writes Hugo, "as a drop of rain slips down a window-pane, rush to the two executioners with the swiftness of a cat which has fallen from a roof, knock them down with two enormous

Notre-Dame de Paris, 1790

fists, pick up the gypsy with one hand, as a child would her doll, and dash back into the church with a single bound, lifting the young girl above his head and crying in a formidable voice, 'Sanctuary!'"

Notre-Dame de Paris was an instant and continuing success. It has never been out of print. As Hugo hoped, its popularity rekindled public interest in the cathedral. "There are two aspects to a building," he wrote. "Its function and its beauty. The function is owned by those who use it, but its beauty belongs to the world."

In 1848, Louis-Napoleon replaced Louis Philippe on the throne and, in 1852, as Emperor Napoleon III, ordered Baron Georges-Eugène Haussmann to begin the mammoth task of modernizing Paris. Inspired by Hugo, the architect Eugène Viollet-le-Duc rebuilt the pointed central spire or *fleche* (literally "arrow") that was demolished by revolutionaries in 1792. He also replaced the heads the anti-royalists broke off the statues on the cathedral's imposing frontage, which they assumed were kings rather than saints.

He also, controversially, made "improvements," adding to the rooftop bronze statues of the twelve apostles, one of whom is a portrait of Viollet-le-Duc himself. Feeling the building needed to be more "Gothic," in the spirit of Hugo, he commissioned a series of gargoyles; stone monsters that stare over the city as Quasimodo does in the novel. These changes had their critics. "When we restore a medieval manuscript," wrote one historian, "we leave blank the parts we can't read: we don't insert new words." The public had no such qualms. The bright new stonework and gleaming statuary reflected a national optimism, snuffed out when Napoleon III led France into a disastrous war with Prussia in 1870.

Like many, Hugo lost his admiration of the monarchy and embraced the republican cause, but his devotion to the great buildings of France never faltered. By the time he died in 1885, his novels, including *Les Misérables*, had made him world-famous. But his monument is *Notre-Dame de Paris* and the inspired invention of Quasimodo – proof that the most despised of creatures can harbour nobility and romance.

The Enduring Myth of the Hunchback

The French regarded *kyphosis*-sufferers ambivalently, even into the 20th century. To rub the back of a sufferer supposedly gave good luck, particularly when it came to money. People with the handicap were common around casinos, where they charged a fee for the service. In Alexandre Dumas's novel *Le Bossu*, the hero pretends to be a hunchback in order to become the accountant of his enemy.

The complex make-up and emotional range of Quasimodo has attracted numerous actors to play the role on stage and in cinema, including Lon Chaney, Charles Laughton, Anthony Quinn and Anthony Hopkins. A sentimental animated version of the story was released by Disney in 1996.

SEE IT: NOTRE-DAME DE PARIS

Located on the eastern half of the Île de la Cité, the Cathedralé Notre-Dame de Paris is an enduring landmark of the city, and one of its most visited sites. The cathedral is open every day of the year. For those with the energy to climb the 387 steps to the top, the South Tower offers close-up views of the roof and Viollet-le-Duc's "improvements," including the *fleche* and the gargoyles.

For more information visit **www.notredamedeparis.fr**.

LA·DAME·
AUX·CAMELIAS

SARAH BERNHARDT

CHAPTER 9

A LA DAME AUX CAMÉLIAS
MARIE DUPLESSIS

Few lives burn brightly enough to ignite a masterpiece. How much more remarkable that a girl who died in 1847, aged only 23, should have inspired many. From Violetta in *La Traviata* to Marguerite Gautier in *La Dame aux Camélias* and its numerous stage and screen incarnations, including that of Greta Garbo in *Camille*, Marie Duplessis came to symbolize the fluttering of the moth as it circled ever closer to the flame.

Though she would die in luxury, Marie's childhood in a Normandy village was squalid. Born Alphonsine Rose Plessis in 1824, she had a prostitute for a grandmother and a priest for a grandfather. Her father, Marin Plessis, was a violent alcoholic. After he set the house on fire, her mother took a job as maid to an English family, sending her two daughters to a cousin. Too poor to feed them, he sent them out to beg.

Even at 10 years old, Alphonsine's pale face and large dark eyes, framed in a cascade of black hair, attracted attention—a fact not lost on her father, who reclaimed the girls when their mother died. Once Alphonsine lost her virginity at 12 to a farm boy, Plessis began boarding her out to lonely bachelor land-owners in need of a "maid." Though such arrangements were commonplace, her father's bartering became too flagrant. When the parish authorities took an interest, he hurriedly sent her to live with relatives in Paris.

First working as a laundress, then as a seamstress, Alphonsine learned to survive in the city. She also contracted tuberculosis, a disease epidemic in Paris's crowded tenements, exacerbated by exhaustion and poor nutrition. It killed every second person infected, but those with money lived longer. The realization of her illness nudged Alphonsine towards one of the few careers open to a pretty but illiterate girl—that of a mistress or *courtisane*.

Marie Duplessis by Édouard Viénot

Her first *protecteur*, a widowed restaurateur named Nollet, spotted her in the Palais-Royal, the enclosed garden next to the Comédie-Française, famous as a pick-up spot. He was in his 50s; she was 15. He rented her an apartment on rue de L'Arcade, a discreet street behind the church of the Madeleine—not fashionable, but at least on the more chic right bank of the Seine.

Her maid also acted as Nollet's spy, but Alphonsine easily gave her the slip. The teenager with the enchantingly vulgar Norman accent was soon a familiar face at the Opéra and the private salons where the fashionable met. Her friend, the actress Judith Bernat, described her as "very slim, almost thin, but wonderfully delicate and graceful; her face was an angelic oval and her dark eyes had a caressing melancholy; her complexion was dazzling. She had an incomparable charm."

In this elegantly amoral society, men about town sampled the latest women as routinely as they patronized new restaurants. Once they chose a woman to keep, these men spent fortunes on clothes, jewels and a smart apartment. A well-kept mistress was as much an ornament to one's reputation as an elegant carriage and a team of beautiful horses. *Les grandes horizontales* competed shamelessly for wealthy clients. The notorious Cora Pearl, a contemporary of Alphonsine, danced nude on a carpet of orchids, bathed before her guests in champagne and, as the climax to a dinner party, was served up nude on a platter.

By contrast, Alphonsine dressed demurely, but always with her trademark flower, a white camellia, on her gown. Her strategy worked. Bored by bold glances and plunging necklines, Antoine Agénor, Duc de Gramont et de Guiche, was drawn to her reticence and reserve. He installed her in a vast apartment on boulevard de Madeleine, filled it with antique furniture from before the Revolution, bought her jewels and a carriage, paid for clothes from the best *couturiers*, and hired servants to cater to her. He also commissioned a portrait from the fashionable painter Édouard Viénot. It shows her as she had been dressed when he first saw her: in a lacy white gown decorated with her emblematic camellia.

The real transformation, however, was intellectual. Even at 18, Alphonsine had a shrewd sense of what was required by the new world into which de Guiche had ushered her. She changed her name to the more discreet Marie, and added "du" to Plessis, hinting at aristocratic ancestry. She decided to learn to read—a rare accomplishment at the time, particularly among women. Charmed, de Guiche persuaded his own grandmother to teach her. Marie's weekly salon became famous for conversation. She entertained writers like Théophile Gautier, Eugène Sue and Honoré de Balzac, attended the opera on the arm of a succession of fashionable men and took the air each afternoon in her carriage in the Bois de Boulogne.

Even in this life of luxury, Duplessis wasn't happy. Her despair was at least partly a symptom of tuberculosis. Another victim, the poet Percy Bysshe Shelley, had written, "I could lie down like a tired child, And weep away the life of care." Sickness also heightened the need for sensation. She gambled extravagantly, ordered whole wardrobes of clothes, bought the most expensive *objets d'art*. Once de Guiche moved on, it took seven *protecteurs* to keep her in this style. She allocated each a day of the week. As it would have been vulgar to show jealousy, the men jointly purchased a bureau

Marie Duplessis, inspiration for *La Dame aux Camélias*, on her deathbed.

with seven drawers in which to keep a change of clothes.

Chance introduced Duplessis to the man who would make her immortal. In 1842, both she and the young Alexandre Dumas were 18. She was the highest-priced of Paris's *poules de luxe* while he was the illegitimate and apparently untalented son of the man who wrote *The Three Musketeers* and *The Count of Monte Cristo*. The two met again two years later, and Duplessis, charmed by Dumas's adoration, admitted him to her bed.

It was a mistake. Unlike her aristocratic admirers, Dumas was jealous and possessive. He insisted on becoming her sole *protecteur*, spent every penny he owned, borrowed more, then lost everything trying to win at baccarat. After this, he persuaded her to live with him in his father's country house, where, he argued, the air would be better for her diseased lungs. For a while Duplessis enjoyed surviving on "love and fresh water," but she soon missed the Opéra, the casinos and the admiration of her lovers. The affair with Dumas lasted only from September 1844 to August 1845. At the end, he wrote to her bitterly, "My Dear Marie, I am neither rich enough to love you as I could wish nor poor enough to be loved as you wish."

Back in Paris, Duplessis married her richest admirer, Count Édouard de Perregaux. It didn't last, and she returned to her self-destructive ways. Her final year was spent in desperate pursuit of a cure, even experimenting with Mesmerism, an early form of hypnotism. When she died at 23, scores of admirers attended her funeral in the cemetery of Montmartre. She died penniless, however, and was buried without a monument. De Perregaux had the body moved to a better site and placed a memorial over her grave.

Her death inspired Dumas. Within five months, he completed the novel he called *La Dame aux Camélias*. Marie became Marguerite Gautier, a courtesan who surrounds herself with camellias. Dumas was Armand Duval, the innocent who, knowing nothing of her reputation, falls in love with her. They run away to the country, but his father begs Marguerite to give him up rather than let him ruin his life. She does so, turning him vengeful. By the time he learns of her sacrifice, she's dying.

Only a modest success as a novel, the story became a hit when Dumas adapted it for the stage. France's greatest actress Sarah Bernhardt agreed to play Marguerite. As an opening night gift—and, some said, an act of revenge—Dumas gave her the letter of renunciation he'd written to Duplessis, recovered when her possessions were sold to pay her debts.

"We are different from other women," Duplessis once told a friend. "We don't own ourselves." Freedom came only in death. In 1853, Giuseppe Verdi adapted *La Dame aux Camélias* into *La Traviata*—literally "The Woman Who Has Gone Astray." In one of the most delirious moments in all of opera, his heroine, the courtesan Violetta Valéry, waltzes through the luxury apartment financed by her multitude of lovers, swearing she'll spend her remaining years in search of pleasure and, above all, *sempre libera*—always free.

SEE IT: MARIE DUPLESSIS'S PARIS

The shade of Marie Duplessis lies lightly on the city that made her famous. Most of the buildings in which she lived were demolished in the modernization of the city by Baron Georges-Eugène Haussmann in the 1850s. Aside from her grave in the 15th division of the Montmartre Cemetery, she has no monuments. Dumas is buried nearby. Duplessis's grave is almost always decorated with fresh camellias.

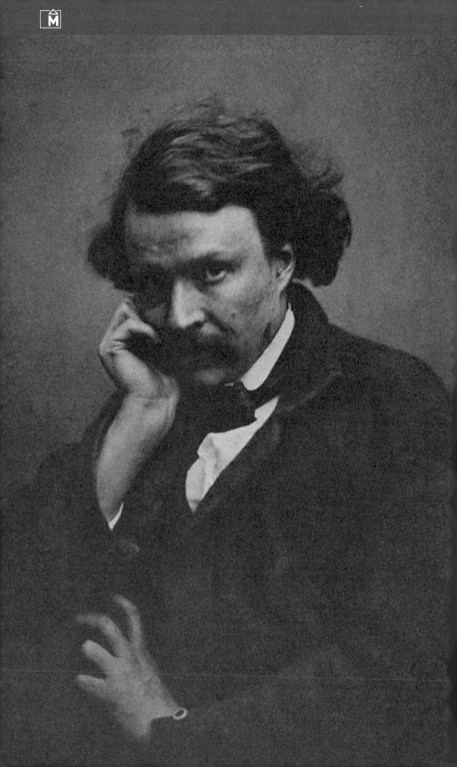

CHAPTER 10.

THE DIVINE CREATOR
THE ECCENTRIC CAREER OF FÉLIX NADAR

Few inventions so transformed society in the mid-19th century as photography. It made the faces of celebrities known to everyone and allowed travelers to offer proof of the wonders they encountered. Linked to a microscope, it could show the tiniest things on earth, while a camera in a balloon gave a view of the world formerly available only to god.

One man exploited these possibilities more than most. Gaspard-Félix Tournachon, better known as Félix Nadar, was born in Paris in 1820. His explosive and self-dramatising personality was emphasised by a mass of red hair and a bushy moustache. He studied medicine, but gave it up when his father's publishing company went bankrupt. He turned his flair for drawing into a job as caricaturist for the comic weekly *Le Charivari*, using his childhood nickname, "Nadar." By 1849, he owned two comic magazines of his own, *Revue Comique* and the *Petit Journal pour Rire*.

In 1854, he created his first "Panthéon Nadar," a huge lithograph incorporating caricatures of numerous prominent Parisians. In preparation for a second in the series, he photographed some of his subjects, including his friends the illustrator Gustave Doré and poet Charles Baudelaire. "The

Adrien Tournachon (Nadar Jeune) by
Felix Nadar, 1854-60

portrait I do best," he said, "is of the person I know best." Photographers of the time often required their subjects to remain immobile for long periods, sitting stiffly in a chair or leaning against a column or pillar. Some even kept them still by locking a metal clamp round their necks. By using shorter exposures and dispensing with props and painted backdrops, Nadar achieved a relaxed naturalism. Impressed, a banker friend offered to set him up as a portrait photographer.

Rather than give up his magazines, Nadar persuaded his brother Adrien, a failed painter and mediocre businessman, to get the studio going. Adrien took lessons with photographer Gustave Le Gray—then told his brother he had no need of him. He could do it all himself. With Le Gray and some other photographers, Adrien then set up shop in a glassed rooftop studio on Paris's fashionable boulevard des Capucines.

Irritated, Nadar built a darkroom in his apartment and experimented with emulsion-coated glass plates that made possible sharper pictures and multiple prints. Like his friend, the science fiction writer Jules Verne, he was excited by technology. Of all the newest inventions—the phonograph, the telegraph, the discoveries in medicine—photography impressed him most. "It seems to finally endow man himself with the divine power of creation," he wrote, "the power to give physical form to the insubstantial image that vanishes as soon as it is perceived, leaving no shadow in the mirror, no ripple on the surface of the water."

As incompetent a photographer as he had been a painter, Adrien was soon floundering. In September 1854, he begged his brother for help. Just married and short of money himself, Nadar used 6,000 francs of his wife's dowry to save the studio. Once Félix began working there, the business picked up. By January 1855, it was back in profit—whereupon Adrien announced he was starting up on his own again, styling himself Nadar *Jeune* (Nadar

George Sand (1864), Sarah Bernardt (c. 1860) and Camille Corot (c. 1860) by Nadar

the Younger). Even worse, he entered a series of Félix's photographs in the Universal Exhibition of 1855 as Nadar *Jeune*, and won a gold medal. Furious, Félix sued to retrieve his name.

Adrien did no better as Nadar *Jeune* than he had as his brother's partner. Just as he opened for business, Andre Disdéri patented a method of taking eight photographs on a single plate, producing multiple prints known as *cartes-de-visite* or visiting cards. Once Emperor Napoleon III posed for a *carte-de-visite*, everyone wanted one. The market for large formal portraits, to be framed on the piano or mantel, melted away in favour of albums into which one could slot hundreds of the smaller pictures. By the time Félix won his lawsuit in 1859, Adrien was bankrupt again.

Félix moved back onto the boulevard des Capucines. Ever the showman, he painted the building red and hung a 50-foot sign across the frontage reproducing the signature for which he'd fought. He was soon once again the pre-eminent society portraitist of Paris. Clients included the writer George Sand, actress Sarah Bernhardt and the painter Camille Corot. "What can [not] be learned," explained Félix, " is the moral intelligence of your subject; it's the swift tact that puts you in communion with the model, makes you size him up, grasp his habits and ideas."

Increasingly, however, he left day-to-day work to assistants or his son Paul while he restlessly experimented with subjects and locations. He made some provocative female nudes and pioneered the use of artificial light, taking electricity for the first time into the catacombs and photographing the corridors lined with human bones.

Most adventurously of all, he took up ballooning. In 1858, he made the first photographs ever taken from the air and in 1863 built *Le Géant* ("The Giant"), a balloon 6,000 cubic meters in volume and 100 meters in circumference. Underneath dangled a wicker gondola, four meters high, which held four beds, a toilet, a darkroom and a lithographic press so that news reports could be printed and thrown to the ground. Once it landed, wheels allowed it to be towed by horses.

Nadar by Honré Daumier, 1862

Le Géant inspired Jules Verne to write *Five Weeks in a Balloon* and to base the character of Michael Ardan in *From the Earth to the Moon* on his friend. The two men formed The Society for the Encouragement of Aerial Locomotion by Means of Heavier than Air Machines. Nadar launched a magazine, *L'Aeronaute*, published a small book, *The Right to Fly*, and envisaged a world in which everyone traveled by balloon.

But *Le Géant* had numerous technical problems and flew only twice. The second time, on October 18, 1863, it carried nine passengers, including Nadar's wife. In 17 hours, it got as far as Nienburg, near Hanover in Germany, a distance of about 400 miles, but as it tried to land, a strong wind dragged it across the ground for seven or eight miles, injuring everyone. Discouraged, Nadar showed *Le Géant* in Brussels and at Britain's Great Exhibition in 1863, but it never flew again.

While his son continued the photography business, Nadar spent most of his time until his death in 1910 writing wordy and unrevealing memoirs. He did, however, earn one more entry in the history books. In April 1874, a group of young painters, rejected by the major salons where new work was traditionally exhibited, decided to hold their own show, and asked to use Nadar's studio. No artists had ever defied the establishment in this way, and Nadar, always the rebel, agreed. In a parody of business terminology, the group called itself *Le Société Anonyme des artistes, peintres, sculpteurs, graveurs, etc* (The Limited Company of Painters, Sculptors, Engravers, etc.) Not until 1877 did they officially adopt the term with which some described that first body of work : Impressionism.

SEE IT: NADAR'S STUDIO

Nadar's studio once stood at 35, boulevard des Capucines (9th *arrondissement*). He is celebrated by Square Nadar (18th), in front of the Basilique du Sacré-Cœur in Montmartre, to the left as you emerge from the funicular.

Some of his photographs are in the Musée d'Orsay, including the portrait of the mime Dubureau with a camera that won the gold medal at the Universal Exhibition when entered in Adrien Tournachon's name.

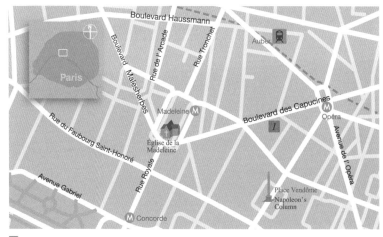

1 Nadar Studio: 35, boulevard des Capucines

CHAPTER 11

THE NIGHT THEY ATE ELEPHANT

THE SIEGE OF PARIS

In 1870, a long-festering tension between France and the Kingdom of Prussia, soon to be part of a unified Germany, erupted into war. France was no match for the efficient and warrior-like Prussians, who overran the army of Emperor Napoleon III and, in September, besieged Paris.

The Siege lasted for five months. Foreign journalists trapped in the city were able to send out reports by balloon. Letters were photographed, reduced to micro-dots, and carried by hot-air balloons launched from the heights of Montmartre. These drifted south, to Tours and Poitiers, where the letters were retrieved, restored to readable size and posted. The balloons also carried pigeons, trained to fly back to Paris carrying similarly miniaturized documents in capsules on their legs. In this way, 150,000 official letters and a million private messages were exchanged.

As the Siege dragged on, the greatest threat to the pigeon post came not from the Prussians but from hungry Parisians. Food prices had already soared by 25 percent before the Siege. By October 1870, pork, beef and mutton were running out fast and butchers began to recommend horse. *Boucheries chevalines*—horse butchers—sprang up, signified by a gilded

A Soup Kitchen during the Siege of Paris, by Henri Pille, after 1870

horse's head above the door. An estimated 70,000 horses were eaten during the Siege, even by the Emperor himself. Two thoroughbreds, a gift of Tsar Alexander II of Russia, provided a number of tasty meals for the imperial court.

Paris had no more distinguished restaurant than Voisin's at 261, rue Saint-Honoré. Its food was famous, but so was its cellar of red wines. "The man who knew the wine list of Voisin's thoroughly," wrote one gourmet, "would be the greatest authority in the world on claret." This quality didn't come cheap; a meal in this modest-looking little restaurant could cost a fortune. "I always chuckle over a tale of three young Englishmen," said one client, "who, coming to Paris for the first time, thought that they had discovered Voisin's. They fancied that all the other English who had been to the French capital had overlooked this quiet restaurant with windows cloaked by lace curtains in the sleepy rue Saint-Honoré, and that they were likely to obtain a rough but well-cooked bourgeois meal there at quite a nominal price. The various stages of their disillusionment were amusing."

Rules at Voisin's were strict. An Englishman who demanded a plum pudding at Christmastime was indignantly refused, as was an American woman who asked for nothing but a salad. "Madame," the maître d', M. Bellanger, icily replied, "this is a restaurant, not a meadow."

Even with the city under siege, Voisin's didn't lower its standards. French cooks were famous for their ability to transform the most banal raw materials, and the restaurant was fortunate to have a chef who regarded the shrinking supplies as a challenge. Alexandre-Étienne Choron came from Caen, in the northern region of Normandy, and was no stranger to simple ingredients. For *Tripes à la mode de Caen,* a specialty of his hometown, pieces of cow's stomach are stewed with onions, herbs and garlic.

Though dogs, cats and rats were available, Choron knew his discriminating clientele would demand something more exotic. In December, his patience was rewarded when Paris's zoo, the Jardin d'Acclimatation, announced it could no longer feed its animals and reluctantly offered them for sale as livestock.

Killing an Elephant for Food in the Jardin des Plantes, from the *Illustrated London News*, 1871

Deer, antelopes and other herbivores were snapped up immediately, as was bear, since their meat, if not familiar, was at least known to more adventurous gourmets. M. Deboos of the Boucherie Anglaise on boulevard Haussmann bought a yak; under all that hair, it was, after all, just a kind of buffalo.

Optimistically, the zoo management offered a hippopotamus at 80,000 francs but found no takers; who knew if the beast was even edible? Lions and tigers were left alone. Nobody wanted the job of killing them. Monkeys, too, were considered too like human beings to be sacrificed; eating them would be like cannibalism.

For his largest purchase, M. Deboos paid 27,000 francs for two elephants, Castor and Pollux. Not sure how to slaughter them, he hired a marksman to shoot the animals with steel-tipped explosive bullets. The purchase turned out to be a bargain. He sold the trunks, the tenderest part, for 40 or 45 francs a pound, the rest for about 10 to 14 francs a pound. Most buyers were disappointed by the taste. Thomas Gibson Bowles, who sent regular dispatches to the English press, wrote that he'd eaten camel, antelope, dog, donkey, mule and elephant and, of those, liked elephant least. Another journalist, Henry Labouchère, reported, "Yesterday, I had a slice of Pollux for dinner. It was tough, coarse and oily. I do not recommend English families to eat elephant as long as they can get beef or mutton."

But Choron, like any great chef, looked on these unpromising ingredients as a challenge. For a midnight Christmas dinner in 1870, Voisin's proposed a meal that has become legendary. This was the menu:

Starters
Butter, radishes, stuffed donkey's head, sardines

Soups
Purée de Red Beans with croutons
Consommé d'Éléphant

Entrées
Fried baby catfish
Roasted camel, English style
Kangaroo Stew
Bear chops with pepper sauce

Roasts
Haunch of wolf with venison sauce
Cat, flanked by Rats
Watercress salad

Antelope Terrine with truffles
Cepes mushrooms Bordelaise style
Green peas with butter

Sweets
Rice pudding with preserves

Dessert
Gruyère cheese

To wash down these exotic dishes, the restaurant offered Mouton-Rothschild 1846, Romanée-Conti 1858, Château Palmer 1864 and, as a digestif, Grand Porto 1827. There was nothing apologetic about this meal. To those privileged to attend, it was the best possible response to the German shells that were reducing the outskirts of Paris to rubble. No amount of high explosive could destroy the French love of food.

Thanks to Choron's ingenuity, the clients at Voisin's developed a taste for elephant. After Christmas, he bought the animal owned by the Jardin des Plantes for 15 francs a pound. Elephant Trunk *in Sauce Chasseur* and *Éléphant bourguignon*—Elephant cooked in red wine—went on the menu. By January 13, however, the meat was used up, and he was forced to substitute horse. Fortunately for Choron, and for any surviving elephants, Napoleon III capitulated at the end of January, and abandoned his throne, along with the contested region of Alsace-Lorraine between Germany and France—a gesture that rankled the French for generations and contributed to two world wars. It's ironic, but also very French, that one of the events most remembered about the Siege was the night the patrons of Voisin's ate camel, wolf and elephant.

Voisin's, already famous, became more so after the Siege, in part because of Choron's banquet. "If the owner looks upon you with eyes of favour," wrote one client, "you will be presented by him with a little pink card, folded in two, on which is the menu of a dinner given at Voisin's on Christmas Day 1870." During the Belle Époque, at the turn of the century, it was a favorite restaurant of the Prince of Wales, Queen Victoria's obese and sensual son and heir, and writers like Alphonse Daudet, Émile Zola and the Goncourt Brothers, publishers who inaugurated the Prix Goncourt, France's most prestigious literary prize. Choron lived until 1924 and, aside from the 1870 dinner, is best known for the invention of Sauce Choron, a form of hollandaise coloured with tomato purée.

A TASTE OF PARIS'S PAST

Voisin's closed in 1930, and the former site, at the corner of rue Saint-Honoré and rue Cambon, is no longer a restaurant. However a few modern establishments maintain the discreet 19th-century ambiance and decor. These include Allard, on rue Saint-André des Arts, near Place Saint-Michel; Le Bon Saint-Pourçain, on rue Servandoni, between Place Saint-Sulpice and the Luxembourg Gardens; and Le Square Trousseau, on rue Antoine Vollon, behind the Opéra Bastille.

Map 1

 Allard: 41, rue Saint-André-des-Arts

2 Le Bon Saint-Pourçain: 10, rue Servandoni

Map 2

3 Le Square Trousseau:
  1, rue Antoine Vollon

CHAPTER 12

ARISE, YOU WRETCHED OF THE EARTH

THE PARIS COMMUNE

For two months in the spring of 1871, the armies of Prussia and its allies besieged Paris. Saint-Cloud and other outer suburbs were bombarded to rubble. The city was starving. The rich ate the animals from the zoo, while the poor survived on dogs, cats and rats. Once all the horses were eaten, many merchants could no longer function. Factories and shops closed. Craftsmen pawned their tools to buy food.

Emperor Napoleon III had foolishly gone to war hoping to restore France's waning influence in Europe, but the Prussians won every battle and even captured the emperor, releasing him on the condition that he retire to England. The elected government fled south to Bordeaux, where it negotiated a capitulation that surrendered the precious border territory of Alsace Lorraine. As the Prussians announced their plan for a victory parade through Paris, the outnumbered French army retreated to Versailles, a dozen miles away. Parisians, convinced they would be slaughtered, collected money to buy 400 cannons, which they stationed on the hill of Montmartre. At the same time, citizens banded together to form a National Guard of 24,000 men, which swelled to 350,000 as the Prussians approached.

‹ *The Arrest of Louise Michel*, by Jules Girardet, 1883

The Cannons of Montmartre During the Paris Commune, 1871

But the citizens' fears were never realized. The invaders behaved with decorum, then returned to Prussia. Paris found itself a free city of ordinary working men and women, with the arms to defend it.

On March 18, French Army troops under generals Claude-Martin Lecomte and Jacques-Léonard Clément-Thomas arrived from Versailles to re-occupy the city and seize the 400 cannons. Soldiers were ordered to fire on those who resisted. Most soldiers, however, were Parisians. As they tried to tow the cannons away, a group of women, led by Louise Michel, the anarchist schoolteacher later called the "Red Virgin of Montmartre," dissuaded them. When the National Guard arrived, most of the troops mutineed and pulled Lecomte and Clément-Thomas from their horses.

"Soldiers broke the windows of the room where General Lecomte was confined," wrote one witness, "threw themselves upon him, dragging him towards the garden. This man who, in the morning, had three times given the order to fire upon the people, wept, begged for pity and spoke of his family. He was forced against the wall and fell under the bullets."

Clément-Thomas was shot shortly after. Those troops that didn't join the rebels fled in confusion.

The Parisians were stunned by the speed of events. The impasse was finally broken when former lieutenant Paul-Antoine Brunel—imprisoned for helping Socialist Louis-Auguste Blanqui's attempt to overthrow the provisional government in October 1870—was released by the National Guard. Taking command, he raided the Prince-Eugène Barracks, capturing the leaderless troops left behind in the retreat. Then he escorted the head of the Guard, Jean Bellevois, to the deserted Hôtel de Ville, Paris's town hall and the symbol of municipal power.

"That evening we did not know what to do," recalled one Guard member. "We did not want possession of the Hôtel de Ville. We were very embarrassed by our authority." News spread of the coup and Brunel was joined at the Hôtel de Ville by Émile Duval, Émile Eudes and other firebrands, many of whom had also been involved in the failed Blanqui uprising. They found National Guardsmen and French Army soldiers milling about while Marxists, republicans and anarchists argued.

Brunel and the Blanqui-ists favored marching on Versailles and attacking the demoralised army, but calmer voices, in particular writer Edouard-Auguste Moreau, persuaded the National Guard to remain in the Hôtel de Ville and hold elections for a city government. The decision was rational but proved disastrous; it gave the national army time to regroup.

Elections on March 26 produced the 92-member Communal Council. With this act, Paris became a commune, an autonomous state ruled by its citizens, called Communards. As president, they chose Blanqui, even though he was in prison. Despite efforts to exchange him for Georges Darboy, archbishop of Paris, he remained incarcerated throughout the period of the Commune.

The Council, which included few professional politicians or administrators, concentrated on practicalities. To get people back to work, moneylenders were forced to return tools pawned by craftsmen. Where the owners of a business had fled, workers were authorised to take over. All debt was suspended for 90 days at zero interest. Pensions were granted to the widows of National Guardsmen killed in the fighting.

Gustave Courbet by Nadar

Next, the Council dealt with long-standing injustices. Bakers would no longer be forced to work all night so that Parisians could have their fresh morning baguettes. Free soup kitchens, called *marmites,* were set up for the poor. Women, well represented in the council, demanded the right to vote, an end to prostitution and the recognition of "common-law" marriages and illegitimate children.

As in the Revolution of 1789, the Catholic Church, a staunch supporter of the state, became a target. All church property was seized, including schools, in which a secular curriculum was introduced. Churches were allowed to remain open only if citizens could also use them for political meetings.

Intellectuals and artists welcomed the Commune. For the first time, the art works of the Louvre—until then reserved for royal eyes—were seen by the public. Opera, theater and music were performed outdoors, and for free. The painter Gustave Courbet was placed in charge of museums and art galleries and was able to prevent their desecration.

Before the war, Napoleon III had offered Courbet the *Légion d'honneur*. Courbet refused. "When I am dead," he announced, "let this be said of me: 'He belonged to no school, to no church, to no institution, to no academy, least of all to any regime except the regime of liberty.'" Courbet particularly disliked the column on Place Vendôme celebrating the victories of Napoleon I. The outside was covered in 425 sculpted bronze plates, melted down from the cannons of armies the emperor had defeated. Courbet persuaded the Communards to demolish it.

On May 23, the government sent a new army under General Patrice MacMahon, Duke of Magenta, to retake the city. His troops had been brought in from the south, around Marseilles, and had no loyalty to Paris. The Communards built 500 barricades from the rubble of buildings demolished by the Prussians and prepared to fight. In a final act of defiance, they executed hostages, including the Archbishop of Paris.

Communard Barricade, 1871

Councilman Jules Bergeret ordered the destruction of all buildings symbolizing the Napoleonic administration. The palace of the Tuileries, the Hôtel de Ville, the Ministry of Finance, the Council of State, the Palace of the Légion d'honneur and the High Court were all set on fire, as were parts of the Louvre. Damage was negligible, except for the Tuileries Palace. It burned for 48 hours, leaving only the shell.

The first Communards died on the summit of Montmartre when the French Army, admitted by a traitor, blew up the gypsum mines into which the Communards had retreated. Amateurs of the National Guard were no match for MacMahon's troops. By the end of May, the last had surrendered or fled. In what became known as the *Semaine Sanglante* (Bloody Week), thousands were executed without trial in the Luxembourg Gardens and at Père Lachaise Cemetery, where, on one occasion, more than 100 men, women and children were shot against what became known as the *Mur des Fédérés* or Communards' Wall.

Mur des Fédérés, 1871

Of the 12,500 Communards actually brought to trial on charges of treason and insurrection, about 10,000 were convicted, mostly on little or no evidence. "In Paris, everyone is guilty!" a prosecutor proclaimed. About 7,500 were jailed, while others, including Louise Michel, were deported to the penal colony of New Caledonia in the South Pacific. The total of murdered Communards is estimated at 20,000. Many were buried on the hill of Montmartre, where the government built the basilica of Sacré-Cœur—not to memorialize the Commune but to "expiate the sins of the Communards" in defying the church and executing Archbishop Darboy.

Paris remained under martial law for five years as the authorities rooted out dissidents. But the spirit of the Commune flourished; it helped inspire the Russian Revolution. *The Internationale*, written by a Communard, became a socialist anthem. Its first lines—"Arise, you prisoners of starvation/Arise, you wretched of the earth"—were known to every Communist.

Gustave Courbet was jailed for six months and fined 500 francs. He was also forced to pay for restoration of the Place Vendôme column, at the rate of 10,000 francs a year for the next 33 years. He died at age 58 in December 1877, a day before the first installment was due.

REMEMBERING THE COMMUNE

The Basilica of Sacré-Cœur is a constant reminder of the Commune. Completed only in 1919, it's regarded as a monument not only to the clergy killed in 1870, but to all martyrs of the Commune and victims of the First World War.

Mur des Fédérés, today

At Père Lachaise, a sculpture marks the *Mur des Fédérés*, where 147 men and women were shot on May 28, 1871, their bodies buried in a common grave. The bronze plates of the Vendôme column were saved, and it is now a landmark of the 1st *arrondissement*. In 1882, Gustave Courbet became the first Communard to be officially honored when a street in the 16th *arrondissement* was named after him.

The *Hôtel de Ville* and other targets of Commune arson were restored. An exception is the Tuileries Palace. After much discussion, the ruins were demolished, as a symbol of imperialism. The site now forms part of the Tuileries Gardens, between the Louvre and the Champs-Élysées.

For those looking to learn more about the Commune, the Musée Carnavalet contains numerous images, including a large collection of photographs.

The association Les Amis de la Commune de Paris maintains an excellent website (in French) with portrait photographs of the Communards, a bibliography, and a section on the women of the Commune. For more information visit **lacomune.perso.neuf.fr**

CHAPTER 13.

THE EMPEROR OF CHEFS
GEORGES AUGUSTE ESCOFFIER

In 1892, César Ritz, manager of London's Savoy Hotel, faced a crisis.
Australian soprano Dame Nellie Melba, about to perform in Wagner's
Lohengrin at Covent Garden, was obsessive about maintaining her voice.
Nothing too hot, too cold or too abrasive must threaten the flow of air
through that priceless throat. However, Dame Nellie liked crunchy toast with
her breakfast and enjoyed a dish of chilly ice cream for dessert.

Ritz put the problem to the hotel's chef and his old friend, Georges
Auguste Escoffier. He was something of a prima donna himself, dapper and
vain, wearing elevated shoes to minimize his shortness. He instinctively
understood Dame Nellie's idiosyncrasies. He had his *sous-chefs* grill a slice
of bread, split it horizontally, then grill it again. The resulting crisp wafer
dissolved on the tongue, with nary a crumb to menace the voice. As for ice
cream, the solution was even simpler. A puree of raspberries, thickened with
arrowroot, created a rose-colored sauce, coating the ice cream and insulating
the singer's throat from any risk of chill. Aware of the value of celebrity
endorsement, Escoffier called his bread creation Melba Toast. The dessert,
with its sauce-covered scoop of vanilla ice cream resembling a peach,
became Peach Melba.

Solving such problems came naturally to Escoffier. He'd been a cook since 13, learning the trade in his uncle's restaurant in Nice. In 1865, at 19, Ulysse Rohant, owner of the Petit Moulin Rouge in Paris, coaxed Escoffier away to become his *commis rôtisseur* (head meat chef) and then *saucier* (creator of sauces). Unlike today's flashy establishments, the great Paris restaurants prided themselves on discretion; Le Petit Moulin Rouge looked dowdy, with lace curtains in the front window, and only a simple painted wooden frontage to advertise its presence.

Dame Nellie Melba

Its culinary demands, however, were stringent. Under Rohant, Escoffier learned all the great dishes invented by cooks of an earlier century like François Vatel and Marie-Antoine Carême. But even as he reproduced complex sauces according to centuries-old recipes, he became increasingly sure that they fit poorly into the pattern of modern eating. These dishes were invented for the aristocracy, who looked on their serving as a form of entertainment. People no longer spent an entire evening eating a meal of a dozen courses, each with its own wine. In a restaurant as much as anywhere else, time was money. Once he had his own restaurant, Escoffier discarded the old *service à la française*, where every dish was placed on the table at the same time, to become cold and unappetising during the course of the meal. He substituted *service à la russe*: Russian-style presentation, where dishes were served in order, each diner receiving his serving at the same moment.

Five years later, Escoffier briefly served in the army during the Franco-Prussian War, becoming *chef de cuisine* to a succession of generals. The grim quality of army food convinced him there was a place in professional cooking for the low-priced, preserved, dried and canned goods then beginning to appear on the market. More importantly, he saw how a kitchen could be organised on military lines. Nobody expected artillerymen to be marksmen. So why must each cook know every dish of the classic repertoire?

Under his system, a group directed by a *saucier* created sauces, a team of *patissieres* did pastry, a *rôtisseur* handled roasts, while apprentices "chopped

César Ritz

their onions"—still the traditional phrase for learning your trade in a well-ordered kitchen. At the head of this *brigade de cuisine*, as he called it, the boss cooked nothing himself but supervised and set the taste and style that distinguished the restaurant. His title, *chef*—chief—became synonymous with the role of the master cook.

Escoffier also imposed military discipline on his staff. Smoking and swearing were banned, as was the bullying of apprentices. He insisted that staff wear long white aprons and the traditional high *toque*, which kept the head cool and prevented sweat and hair finding its way into the food. He also banned drinking on the job, a bane of most kitchens. Instead, he asked a doctor to invent a reviving non-alcoholic drink. The result was barley water, an infusion of barley flavored with lemon. A large container of this drink was a feature of every Escoffier kitchen.

In 1878, Escoffier left Paris and, still only 30, opened Le Faisan Doré (The Golden Pheasant) in Cannes. Two years later, the wily César Ritz, a Swiss hotel manager, persuaded him to take over the kitchens of the Grand Hotel in Monte Carlo in the winter and the Grand National in Lucerne in the summer. In 1888, they opened an additional restaurant in the German resort of Baden-Baden. It attracted the attention of Richard D'Oyly Carte, the London theatrical entrepreneur who used his profits from producing the operas of Gilbert and Sullivan to build the Savoy Hotel. He invited Ritz to become its manager and Escoffier its *chef de cuisine*. Assembling what they called "a little army of hotel men," the two descended on London.

Dinner at Hotel Ritz, by Pierre-Georges Jeanniot, 1904

The Savoy, with its dining room offering spectacular views over the Thames, became their masterpiece. High society no longer held dinner parties at home; it dined at the Savoy.

Ritz and Escoffier ran the hotel from 1889 until 1897. Not that Ritz was there very much. Instead, he buzzed around Europe and North Africa, consulting for other hotels, launching companies to supply them and trading on his reputation as manager of the Savoy. In 1898, the owners complained, "When in London you are hardly ever in the hotel except to eat and sleep. You have latterly been simply using The Savoy as a place to live in, a pied-à-terre, an office, from which to carry on your other schemes and as a lever to float a number of other projects in which The Savoy has no interest whatever."

An audit of the accounts revealed massive irregularities. Ritz and his assistant had stolen wine to the value of £11,000, twenty times that sum in modern terms. Escoffier was no less guilty. He'd accepted kickbacks from vendors and set up his own company to supply goods at inflated prices. He accepted that he owed The Savoy £8,000, but could only pay £500, since he was effectively broke. In March 1898, he and Ritz were dismissed, along with the supplies manager and 16 cooks, who brandished their knives and refused to leave until ejected by the police.

Returning to Paris, Escoffier took over the kitchens of the Ritz-Carlton. A distinguished, diminutive figure with a drooping silver moustache and sweep of white hair, he came to embody the image of the master *cuisinier*. His books *Le Guide Culinaire* and *Ma Cuisine* became bibles of cookery. Ironically, his reputation attracted the attention of the aristocracy and royalty who could afford to commission the kind of lavish banquets he had reacted against as a young chef. Escoffier acquiesced, but sometimes with a hint of the subversive.

For one dinner, everything was pink, from the table decorations of pink and white roses to the meal: *borscht,* a Russian beetroot soup with cream, chicken filets in a sauce coloured with red paprika and baby lamb, served in the French style, pink at the centre. For a 1908 dinner at which the Prince of Wales was the guest of honor, he puckishly created *Nymphes à l'Aurore* (Nymphs In the Dawn). In the depths of a clear champagne jelly, tiny morsels of meat, tinted pale pink, peeped from green fronds in a tantalising suggestion of female thighs wreathed in water plants. Nobody realised that they were enjoying a dish the British traditionally loathed: frogs' legs.

In 1913, after Escoffier served a lunch for 146 people for Kaiser Wilhelm II, the German head of state told him "I am the Emperor of Germany, but you are the Emperor of Chefs." Never one for excess modesty, Escoffier could only agree.

ESCOFFIER'S RECIPE: NYMPHES À L'AURORE

Trim frogs' legs well, poach in white wine and allow to cool in their cooking liquid. When cold, drain and dry carefully. Coat each with a *chaud-froid* sauce (a *béchamel* enriched with egg yolks, cream and gelatin to create a thick glaze) colored with a little paprika.

Cover the bottom of the deep glass dish with a thick layer of aspic made with fish stock, champagne and gelatin. When thoroughly set, lay the glazed frogs' legs on top and decorate with fresh leaves of tarragon and chervil to create the effect of water plants. Cover with another layer of aspic and chill.

For a more dramatic effect, serve the dish on a bed of ice.

CHAPTER 14.

THE OPÉRA GARNIER
ONE MAN'S GLITTERING VISION

In 1875, the Empress Eugenie stared in astonishment at the new Paris opera house that her husband, Emperor Napoleon III, had commissioned as the centrepiece of a rebuilt and modernized Paris.

It certainly filled the eye, dominating the Place de l'Opéra. Its façade was festooned with gilded gods and goddesses, some holding harps and music scores, but all double or triple the size of mere mortals. Above them, a frieze of the names of great composers emphasized that this was a temple to artistic titans.

Eugenie turned to the 35-year-old architect Charles Garnier, who won the competition to design the building from among 171 submissions. "But, Monsieur Garnier!" she said. "The style … it's not Greek. It's not Roman. It's not Gothic. What style is it?"

Reputations have foundered on lesser questions. Garnier could hardly admit that his design was a hodgepodge of elements from the Italian Baroque, garnished with copies of classical sculpture. But he understood the crucial

Opéra de Paris, 1875

Charles Garnier

role of vanity in dealing with a client. "Why, your imperial highness," he replied, "it's *your* style!"

In that instant, a new fashion was born. Soon, every architect in Europe was falling over himself to build in the style of the Second Empire.

With his dark curly hair and "artistic" moustache, Charles Garnier looked the very image of the aesthete. The classic self-made man, he'd erased the inconvenient fact that his father, a former blacksmith, ran a carriage rental service on working-class rue Mouffetard. Instead, he announced he was of noble origins, from the region of Sarthe, rich in *châteaux* and ancient abbeys.

At the École Royale des Beaux-Arts de Paris, the precocious Garnier won the Premier Grand Prix de Rome in 1848, at only 23 years old. For the next five years, he traveled through Italy and Greece, busily sketching artifacts of the ancient world—useful material when he entered the 1861 competition to build the new Paris Opéra. His design was judged not so much the most original as the one closest to the Emperor Napoleon's grandiose vision of Paris as an imperial capital.

Until the mid-19th century, opera had been intimate, a diversion of aristocracy. With the arrival of grand opera, however, composers began to think in terms of spectacle. Garnier, using the newest techniques of steel construction, designed what was, in its day, the world's largest opera house.

Productions there would never be cheap, but the more people one could cram in to see them, the more money one made.

Garnier's building had an unprecedented 17 stories, seven of them beneath the stage. It seated 2,200 spectators, many of them in private boxes as large as living rooms. There was space on the 11,000 square meter stage for 450 performers, plus—thanks to a treadmill floor—a team of galloping horses. It took 1,500 permanent employees to service this temple to art and commerce.

The Staircase of the Opéra, by Louis Beroud, 1877

Though the site occupied three acres, only a fifth of that was auditorium. The rest housed the machinery and storage necessary for its ambitious productions, including stables to house the white horses used in lavish spectacles like the battle scenes in the 1827 *Cromwell*.

Not that people attended the Opéra de Paris for the music or even the staging. They went to see others and to be seen by them. Garnier filled the interior with multiple foyers and staircases where one could show off, but also corridors, staircases, niches and alcoves into which couples could slip away to gossip and flirt. Velvet drapes, gold leaf, mosaics and statues of nymphs and shepherds (some of them wearing not much more than a superior smile) stimulated the senses and inspired conversation. As they climbed the branching marble staircase and stepped into the gilded foyer with its blazing chandeliers, its mirrors and statuary, men stood a little taller and women wished they'd worn their diamonds after all.

Courtesans in a private box at the
Opéra Garnier

Not everyone was a fan of Garnier's overture. The composer Claude Debussy growled, "it looks like a railway station. But once you're inside, you'll be more likely to mistake it for a Turkish bath." However, he was in the minority.

Even during performances, theater-goers remained on show. The rich rented a box for the season. These became shop windows where the owner displayed his new wife or mistress, or both, while serving champagne and caviar to a succession of visitors. The most expensive courtesans knew it was good business to be seen in an opera box, where they were more likely to attract the attention of a wealthy protector.

For architects designing new constructions for the surrounding boulevards, Garnier's influence was overwhelming. Boulevard Haussmann, which runs behind the Opéra, became the premiere shopping street in Paris, dominated by two huge department stores, Au Printemps and Galeries Lafayette, both of which boasted lavish appointments in the flowing Art Nouveau style.

Garnier never participated in the fever of new building he'd inspired. Though he designed the Astronomical Observatory at Nice, Paris's Marigny Theatre and the Casino in Monaco, he was conscious that, in the Paris Opéra, he had achieved his masterwork. Retiring to his villa in Italy, he spent the rest of a long life basking in the glory of the high Baroque style he created.

SEE IT: THE OPÉRA AND ITS PHANTOM

In 1990, the Paris Opéra moved to a new purpose-built opera house on Place de la Bastille. Garnier's original, now re-christened the Palais Garnier, became the headquarters of the National Ballet. You can tour the building most days at a modest price. For more information visit **www.operadeparis.fr**.

A creation as grandiose as the Paris Opéra deserves a myth of equal size. In 1910, Gaston Leroux, a mildly successful novelist and former crime reporter, was looking for a good mystery plot. As a journalist, he had visited the cellars of the building, where prisoners were held during the 1871 Commune. At that time, pumps had to run 24 hours a day to hold back water seeping into the foundations. He also recalled that, in 1896, one of the counter-weights supporting the six-ton chandelier in the center of the auditorium broke loose and killed a member of the audience.

The incidents fused in his imagination. What if some lost soul—mad, mutilated, or just despairing—still lurked under the Opéra, moving by boat on a black lake, perhaps, fed from those underground springs? What if this man knew of secret passages into the building, and disrupted a production by cutting loose the chandelier? And then kidnapped a beautiful young singer, carrying her back to his lair? Leroux called his story *Le Fantôme de l'Opéra*, or *The Phantom of the Opera*.

No great success on first publication, it has since inspired numerous films, including the silent-movie portrayal of Lon Chaney and the stage musical of Andrew Lloyd Webber.

Linley Sambourne. 7 rue Yee. Paris June 15

CHAPTER 15

MAN OF IRON

THE TOWER OF GUSTAVE EIFFEL

Alexandre Gustave Eiffel, one of the most innovative engineers of the 19th century, appears never to have smiled. Even in the one light-hearted image that survives, of him posing with his grandchildren in the gondola of a balloon, he's expressionless. Everything about him—clipped beard, stocky frame, pouchy eyes—suggests a man who would always demand "Prove it!" He had five children, but when his wife Marie died in 1877, he moved in with his daughter Claire and never remarried. His life was work.

Unlike Hector Guimard, who designed the flowing Art Nouveau entrances to Paris's Métro, Eiffel never descended to mere decoration. He took pleasure in the bleak, functional beauty of raw, riveted metal. French architects traditionally signed their buildings, chiseling a name and date into the stone. But there is no such signature on the Eiffel Tower, only a modest bust at its base, added much later. One can only repeat the dedication in London's St. Paul's Cathedral to its architect, Christopher Wren: "If you seek his monument, look around you."

Eiffel's German ancestors came to France in Napoleon's time. They settled in Dijon and abandoned their family name, Bönickhausen. Eiffel graduated

Gustave Eiffel, 1888

as a chemist, intending to manage his uncle's vinegar and paint factory. Cheated of the job in a family squabble, he took a minor job with Charles Nepveu, who designed bridges. Cast iron was replacing stone for major construction, and Eiffel saw how bridges in particular could be made lighter and more durable by prefabricating their components and training unskilled workers to bolt them together. Encouraged by Nepveu, Eiffel developed a system of uniform modules with which one could erect a prefabricated building almost anywhere. His method soon became famous. Orders rushed in from the tropics, where heat, humidity and insects attacked stone and wood. Eiffel built a church in Mozambique and a post office in Saigon without visiting either city. Both were made in France, shipped in sections and assembled at the site.

In 1887, Paris announced an Exposition Universelle to commemorate the 1889 centennial of the Revolution. The committee leased the Champ de Mars, a park on the left bank of the Seine used for military parades. The main entrance would be a tower, and a competition was held for its design.

Eiffel was reeling from the scandal surrounding the plan to cut a sea-level canal through the Isthmus of Panama, for which he was to have built the locks. When the company promoting the plan collapsed with enormous losses, Eiffel was partly blamed and tried for fraud, though he was exonerated. The Exposition contest offered a way to salvage his reputation, but he only became interested when two of his engineers, Émile Nouguier and Maurice Koechlin, produced a design for a 300-meter-high tower that would be the world's tallest building. Architect Stephen Sauvestre added some refinements, which Eiffel endorsed; once he also agreed to invest his own money, it became the unanimous choice.

The tower was intended to stand for the period of the Exposition only. Officials chose Eiffel's design, in part, because it would be easy to disassemble. He worked as he had with his bridges, casting 12,000 iron girders and assembling them on the site with 2,500,000 rivets. As each component had to line up precisely, he used a method that went back to ancient Egypt, weighting the four piers of the tower with tons of sand. By removing or adding sand, he could minutely adjust the height of individual piers.

With only 26 months in which to finish the job, Eiffel, a perfectionist, drove his crews remorselessly. Strikes repeatedly delayed construction. There were three floors: the first at 57 meters, the second at 115 meters and the third at 276 meters. A restaurant was built on the first and Eiffel ultimately kept a personal apartment at the summit. As the tower rose, nearby residents became terrified that it would fall on them. Eiffel had to visit them personally to reassure them. Critics too were scathing. It was called "the skeleton of a bell tower," "a truly tragic street lamp," "a piece of gym equipment, incomplete, confused and deformed" and "a giddy, ridiculous tower, dominating Paris like a gigantic black smokestack."

Following the model of London's Great Exhibition of 1851, Paris's Exposition celebrated the achievements of the Industrial Revolution as well as the latest developments in art and entertainment. Sprawling across acres of the left bank, vast halls of glass and metal displayed the fruits of man's mechanical ingenuity. Elsewhere, visitors could enjoy Auguste Rodin's statue *The Kiss* or watch Buffalo Bill and Annie Oakley perform in their *Wild West Show*.

However, Eiffel's tower, acting as the gate to the Exposition, was the runaway success of the event. Demolition was never seriously considered, particularly after he showed its practical advantages—not only as a tourist attraction, but as a site for radio transmitters and aircraft homing beacons, and for jamming enemy transmissions in times of war. Today, every Paris TV and radio station beams from the tower and the entire area of the Champ de Mars has Wi-Fi access.

For the opening, Eiffel hosted a lunch at the tower's restaurant. Thomas Edison was among the guests. Afterwards, they ascended to Eiffel's apartment for brandy and cigars, where Edison presented him with his latest invention, a phonograph. He wrote in the guest book, "To M. Eiffel, the Engineer. The brave builder of so gigantic and original specimen of

G. Eiffel at the summit of the Eiffel Tower, 1887-89

modern Engineering, from one who has the greatest respect and admiration for all Engineers, including the Great Engineer, the *Bon Dieu*." Eiffel's apartment remained closer to God than any other man-made location until 1930, when New York's Chrysler Building became the world's tallest.

Regarded as the greatest of ironmasters, Eiffel was offered prestigious projects, like creating the internal armature to support France's gift to the United States, the Statue of Liberty: essentially a miniature Eiffel Tower within Bartholdi's statue. Having mastered earth-bound construction, he turned to aerodynamics, which had intrigued him from the moment he noted the effect of wind pressure on his bridges. In 1912, past the age when most men retire, the 80-year-old engineer created one of the world's first wind tunnels and began experimenting with the streamlining of buildings and aircraft. In building it, Eiffel made one proviso: once it no longer served a purpose, it should be demolished. Monuments held no interest for him, only the useful.

Today, France without his temporary tower is inconceivable. It has inspired thousands of paintings and numerous filmmakers have used it as a setting. The tower has been repeatedly decorated and illuminated, most recently for the millennium celebrations in 2000, when it was covered with thousands of flickering halogen lights. Intended, like the tower, to be temporary, these survive, but are switched on for only five minutes every hour, on the hour. They proved more successful than other suggestions to celebrate the event, one of which proposed to exploit the tower's resemblance to a gigantic bird by having it lay, as a symbol of the new millennium, a mammoth egg.

SEE IT: EIFFEL'S IMPACT ON PARIS

The Tour Eiffel remains Eiffel's most visible and accessible work. Today, it houses two restaurants; Eiffel's private apartment is a museum, complete with Edison's phonograph. Other examples of Eiffel's work are harder to find. One of the best is the department store Le Bon Marché, designed in 1876 in association with Louis-Charles Boileau, at 24, rue du Sèvres in the 7th *arrondissement*. Its cast-iron columns, glass roofs and delicate balconies survive relatively intact.

The Paradis Latin revue theater at 28, rue du Cardinal Lemoine (5th) was rebuilt by Eiffel between 1887 and 1889. Despite subsequent reconstructions, some elements of his work survive. His wind tunnel, the Aerodynamique Eiffel, still functions, but is not open to the public. The Ruche, or Beehive, a temporary building designed as the wine rotunda for the 1900 Great Exposition, was relocated to Passage Dantzig in the 15th arrondissement and adapted into artists' studios, but has virtually disappeared within new buildings.

One of the best displays of his method is the church of Notre-Dame du Travail at 35, rue Guilleminot, in the 14th, near Place de Catalogne. Its architect, Jules Astruc, a disciple of Eiffel, used iron beams for the interior, hoping to combine the atmosphere of both church and factory.

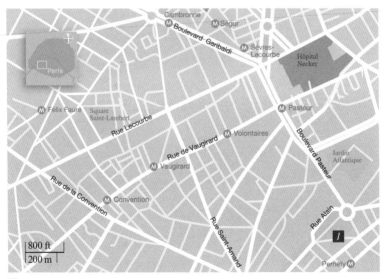

1 Notre-Dame du Travail: 36, rue Guilleminot

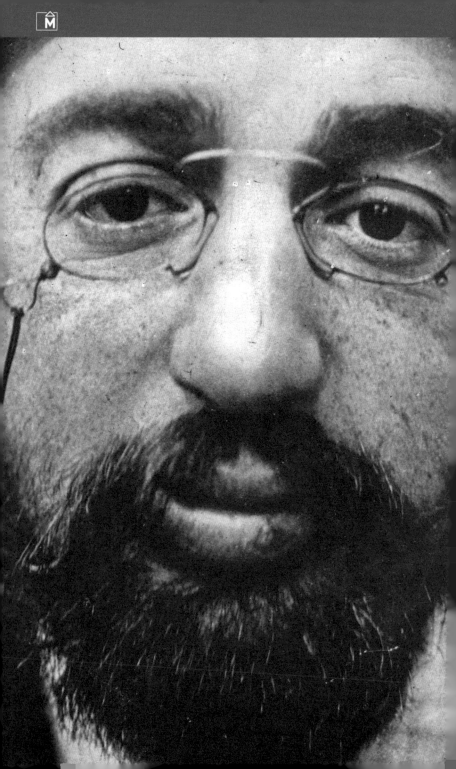

CHAPTER 16

MONTMARTRE AND TOULOUSE-LAUTREC

ARISTOCRAT UNTAMED

As night fell on the Paris of 1895 and the *colleurs d'affiches* trundled down the steep, narrow streets of Montmartre, pushing their iron-wheeled carts loaded with posters, brushes and pots of glue, figures lurked in their wake—not the knife-carrying gangsters whom the people of this lawless hilltop suburb called *apaches* after the American natives, but another sort of thief entirely. The moment the rattle of the cart on the cobbles faded away, they were plucking at the edges of the still-wet posters, peeling them off the wall. A few days later, the stolen images would decorate the studios of connoisseurs who couldn't afford the canvases of this gifted artist.

Just as his friend Vincent van Gogh is remembered as the mad painter who cut off his ear and gave it to a whore, Henri de Toulouse-Lautrec is, to many, the bearded midget in the bowler hat who waddled through the cabarets and brothels of *la Belle Époque*. Yet his work captured nighttime Paris with a vividness nobody has matched—equally immediate and enduring. For Toulouse-Lautrec's secret, one need look no further than the lips. Nobody smiles in a Lautrec picture. Under the gaudy stage make-up or the prostitutes' powder and rouge, the faces are numbed by boredom or darkened by anguish and despair.

Aristide Bruant seen in a poster by Toulouse-Lautrec and a photo

To anguish and despair, Toulouse-Lautrec was no stranger, though he had no expectation of either when he was born, wealthy and aristocratic, to the Comte Alphonse and Comtesse Adèle de Toulouse-Lautrec in the southern city of Albi in 1864. His parents were first cousins, however, and passed on to their children all the genetic weaknesses of inbreeding. A second son died in infancy. At 13, one of Henri's thighbones snapped and, a year later, the other. Neither healed correctly, and though his torso grew normally, he would walk all of his brief life on the legs of a boy. Aware that the marriage was doomed, the Comte abandoned his son's care to his wife. Henri's dying words were a curse on his father: "*Le vieux con,*" the old asshole.

Henri showed his artistic talent early. As a child, he filled sketchbooks with drawings of the horses and servants on his grandfather's estate. A portrait of the artist at 20, painted by his friend Henri Rachou, shows a pale, bespectacled young man with full, sensual lips and a mop of black hair. A nude female torso in the background hints at his erotic nature—a tragic one, since his genetic weakness meant he could never have children, while respectable women shunned him because of his height. He found relief in brothels and in drink—two pleasures that would, ironically, contribute to his death, since prostitutes gave him syphilis, while a taste for absinthe made him an alcoholic.

Yvette Guilbert, 1894

Considering his afflictions, one would expect someone solemn and bitter, but Toulouse-Lautrec was the reverse: charming, humorous (particularly with women) and occasionally childishly playful. He loved fancy dress. He was photographed in the robes of a Japanese priest, a gypsy dancer, an Arab and, least likely of all, wearing the boa and feathered hat of dancer Jane Avril, which clashed with his beard and moustache. Even his drinking was lighthearted. His hollow cane held a glass tube filled with cognac. When American visitors introduced the cocktail to France, he invented his own: the *Tremblement de Terre* or Earthquake, a mixture of cognac and absinthe.

His liking for costume drew him to the theater. He sat in the cabarets of Montmartre night after night, sketching both performers and audience at a table specially reserved for him. Entrepreneurs commissioned images to advertise stars and shows. The singer Yvette Guilbert initially disliked the way he exaggerated her on-stage poses and emphasized her pointed nose, but in time understood his brilliance. In 1894, she agreed to him illustrating a book about her work by Gustave Geffroy. Its cover, showing her trademark long black gloves draped over the edge of the stage next to a forgotten bouquet, became a classic. For songwriter Aristide Bruant, he created posters showing him in his habitual costume: black cloak, wide black hat, red scarf flamboyantly flung over his shoulder. He drew the two stars of the Moulin Rouge, singer Jane Avril and its star dancer Louise Weber, who went by *La Goulue* (The Glutton). Both are caught high kicking in the notorious *can can,* invented by laundresses to show off their snowy petticoats—and the fact that they wore nothing under them.

With such regular work, Henri no longer needed his mother's financial support. Most of his earnings went to prostitutes and drink. Since, after a binge, he frequently woke in a brothel, he took to spending days, even

Toulouse-Lautrec in His Studio, by Maurice Guibert, 1894

weeks in such places, sketching the women before they put on their makeup and took off their clothes. His images provide a unique portrait of the *bordel*, which he shows as an almost entirely female culture. The women, many of them lesbian, regard their life with a bored indifference and their clients with contempt. Vice has never looked so little fun.

For his posters and illustrations, Lautrec worked in charcoal and colored crayon, then transferred the image to lithographic stones, from which hundreds of copies would be made. His speed and lack of precision earned the contempt of colleagues who preferred more finished work. But he knew that what he drew one night might not exist the next. Whores moved on, models disappeared, performers ended their run. Jane Avril, a lesbian, commissioned a poster of her lover, the Irish singer May Belfort, but Belfort died without seeing it.

Just as the cabaret culture existed only for a night, Henri's life was equally brief. As drinking and syphilis further eroded his health, his mother placed him in a sanitarium in Malromé, near Albi. He died there in September

1901, at only 36. Mourned by his bohemian friends, he was regarded by respectable society with contempt. One critic sneered: "The fruits of old family trees are generally weak and, though red, wormy inside. This artist of Montmartre belonged to an exhausted race, and was a caricature of it—weak, shrivelled, counterfeit." But history had the last word; Toulouse-Lautrec has become immortal.

THE LEGACY OF TOULOUSE-LAUTREC

Anyone who dislikes Toulouse-Lautrec will suffer in today's Paris. No artist is more widely reproduced—on postcards, posters, T-shirts, even refrigerator magnets. The museum in Albi holds the largest number of original works, but in Paris, the Musée d'Orsay has a representative collection, including the famous *Rousse - La Toilette* (*Redhead - Bathing*) and *The Clown Cha-U-Kao*.

Mural of Moulin Rouge

Fortunately for the enthusiast, most Lautrec sites are clustered in Montmartre and the 9th and 18th *arrondissements*, including his former studios at 5, avenue Frochot and 21, rue Caulaincourt. Though it's much transformed, the Moulin Rouge still exists at 82, boulevard de Clichy, as does the Folies-Bergère, at 32, rue Richer in the 9th, for which Lautrec designed posters. The former studio of the painter Leon Bonnat at 30, avenue de Clichy (9th *arrondissement*), is now a park, but nearby paved alleys lined with artists' studios retain a flavour of the Lautrec era.

So does the Cirque d'Hiver or Winter Circus, 110, rue Amelot (11th), a permanent building created so that the circus could be offered all year round. Many of Lautrec's circus pictures were inspired by its shows. Georges Seurat's *Le Cirque*, unfinished at his death in 1891 and hanging in the Musée d'Orsay, also shows a typical performance, with acrobats and clowns.

CHAPTER 17

A TOUCH OF THE STRANGE

MAURICE UTRILLO AND THE PAINTERS OF MONTMARTRE

Suzanne Valadon was 18 years old when she gave birth to a son in 1891. The former trapeze artist showed him to the painters she'd modeled for, any of whom might be his father. Auguste Renoir denied responsibility; the baby had none of the pink plumpness associated with his work. Edgar Degas said the child lacked the grace of the ballet dancers that were his favorite subject. But a minor Spanish painter named Miguel Utrillo jumped at the chance to be the boy's father: "I would be glad to put my name to the work of either Renoir or Degas!" When the boy, born Maurice Valadon, was eight years old, Utrillo formally adopted him.

Dominating the skyline of northern Paris, the *butte* or bluff of Montmartre was named for Mars, the Roman God of war, whose temple once stood at the summit. Later, Parisians adapted the name to mean "Mount of Martyrs," to commemorate the *Montmartrois* who died during the brief 1871 socialist uprising of the Commune.

With its winding streets overlooking the city, the district inspires myths and dreamers. From the decapitated Saint-Denis and the rebels of the Commune to the painters of the Belle Époque, it has always had a touch of the strange.

‹ *Portrait of Maurice Utrillo*, Suzanne Valadon, 1921

Montmartre street scene, 1929

Bal-musette Montmartre, by Théophile Steinlen

Originally, Montmartre was a hillside village outside the city, popular with weekend visitors since wine was sold there tax-free. In the middle of the 19th century, Baron Georges-Eugène Haussmann's plan to renovate Paris transformed it. As his crews demolished whole districts of working-class housing—giving wealthy developers the right to erect shops and apartment blocks on the sites—thousands of people, forced from their homes, relocated to Montmartre, covering the slopes with steep, narrow alleys and plunging stone steps.

With its own markets, churches, cemetery and even a vineyard, Montmartre was self-sufficient; it became a refuge for the dispossessed. Prostitutes, abortionists and criminals gravitated there, followed by drug users and their dealers, then political radicals and visionaries. Performers followed. Shortly after, painters and illustrators arrived, attracted by cheap rents and colorful subjects. In particular, Montmartre's cabarets, brothels, *bal musettes* (dance halls) and *guinguettes* (outdoor wine shops) became subjects for a generation of artists including Henri de Toulouse-Lautrec, Auguste Renoir and Vincent van Gogh.

With neither space nor money to construct new buildings, artists lived and worked where they could find room, usually in former commercial spaces. An old windmill became a restaurant, the Moulin de la Galette, where painters such as Renoir ate, drank and worked. Another group took over a one-time piano factory on rue Ravignan. It had neither light nor heating, and in a storm the ancient beams and planks creaked so much that they resembled the floating laundries that bobbed along the Seine. The building became known as the Washerwomans' Boat or Bateau-Lavoir.

Suzanne Valadon (1865-1938) and son Maurice Utrillo, born Maurice Valadon (1883-1955), c. 1889

Tenants included Henri Matisse, Georges Braque, André Derain, Raoul Dufy, Marie Laurencin, Amedeo Modigliani and Pablo Picasso, who made it his home from 1904 to 1909 and kept a studio there until 1912. It was in this rickety ruin that Braque developed Cubism and Picasso painted the controversial *Demoiselles d'Avignon*. The poets Guillaume Apollinaire and Max Jacob added a dash of political intrigue to the area. Apollinaire's incendiary views on art and his involvement in selling some stolen antique stone heads to Picasso made both men suspects in the 1911 theft of the *Mona Lisa* from the Louvre.

The creative excitement spilled onto the streets. Oscar Metenier, a former detective turned writer of pulp novels, converted an abandoned chapel into Paris's smallest theater, the Grand Guignol, which presented plays devoted to horror and sadism. At cabarets such as L'Enfer (Hell) and Le Neant (Nothingness), guests were greeted at the door by a devil wielding a pitchfork. By the light of candlesticks constructed from real human bones, they ate and drank at tables made of coffins.

Lapin Agile

A rundown bar, formerly the Cabaret des Assassins, became Au Lapin Agile (The Frisky Rabbit). With no money for entertainment, guests were invited to sing or otherwise perform for their supper—foreshadowing the coffeehouse poetry readings of the Beat Generation. Such artistic interaction was expected in Montmartre. At Le Chat Noir, the café made famous by Théophile Steinlen's striking posters, the owner published his own literary magazine and delivered satiric monologues to guests, while avant-garde composer Erik Satie served as the resident pianist.

But what about Suzanne Valadon and her son? Their story became a kind of Montmartre fable, a parable of its miseries and joys. Valadon flourished. She took what she learned from her former clients and became a successful painter of unromantically realistic female nudes. She maintained her bohemian lifestyle—wearing a bunch of carrots as a corsage and keeping a goat, to which she fed her unsuccessful drawings. Her lovers included Satie, who proposed marriage after their first night together. When she refused him, he complained that his life became "nothing but an icy loneliness that fills the head with emptiness and the heart with sadness."

Her son, Maurice Utrillo, had his share of misery, too. While Valadon

Portràit of Erik Satie,
Suzanne Valadon, c. 1892

was busy with her art and her lovers, his grandmother took him in. Like many frugal cooks, she followed the custom of *chabrot*— pouring a glass of red wine into the dregs of the soup so as not to waste a mouthful. Because of such habits, Utrillo was an alcoholic by 16. He suffered from mental illness and a compulsion to stalk women. Upon seeing a woman on the street, he would tremble, cry out and seem to be both attracted to and frightened of her in a way that made women flee in terror.

A doctor in the asylum where he was confined suggested painting as therapy. Valadon taught him the basics, then locked him in the upstairs room of their house with a supply of pigment and canvases. He showed a natural talent, but a monomaniac preoccupation with the streets of Montmartre. He would paint nothing else, though always from postcards or memory, since his mother and, later, his wife, learned it was dangerous to let him out unattended. Despite his alcoholism and illness, Utrillo found commercial and critical success, and eventually moved with his wife to a mansion in the village of Sannois—a place with fewer temptations.

As Utrillo, and so many like him, discovered, Montmartre's pleasures and rewards always come with a price. "Happiness," observed one-time *Monmartrois* Amedeo Modigliani, "is an angel with a serious face."

MONTMARTRE: A TRIP BACK IN TIME

The Bateau-Lavoir, today

Of all the districts of Paris, Montmartre is perhaps the least affected by the 21st century. There is little new construction, and the characteristic staircases and alleys have been preserved. Rue Maurice Utrillo (all addresses in the 18th *arrondissement*), actually a cascade of stone steps, is named for the painter. Nearby, a plaque on 5, rue du Mont-Cenis, subject of a famous Utrillo painting, indicates the site of the restaurant La Grande Artiste (currently Les Coulisses) where he and his mother dined frequently from 1919 to 1935. Their home and studio was on nearby rue Cortot.

The original Bateau-Lavoir burned down in 1961 (one year after being declared a National Monument). The site at 13, rue Ravignan, now Place Émile Goudeau, displays a shop-window exhibition of photographs and memorabilia. Auguste Renoir lived at numerous addresses in Montmartre, including 8, allee des Brouillards, which he felt had the best view in all of Paris. Fantasy writer Marcel Aymé lived off rue Norvins on the Place that bears his name. A statue by the actor Jean Marais of a man emerging from a wall commemorates Aymé's 1943 story *Le Passe-Muraille,* or *The Walker-Through-Walls.*

The Grand Guignol Theatre still exists in an alley at 20 bis, rue Chaptal in Pigalle, but is now the International Visual Theatre, directed by the actress Emmanuelle Laborit, deaf since birth, and devoted to productions of plays in sign language.

The Montmartre Cemetery is the final home of numerous celebrities, including authors (Stendahl, Feydeau, Heine), composers (Offenbach,

Delibes, Berlioz), artists (Degas, Picabia, Moreau), performers (Nijinsky, *can can* dancer La Goulue) and filmmakers (Truffaut, Clouzot), as well as society hostess Juliette Récamier, famously painted by David in 1800, and the pioneering chef Careme. Of special interest are Nijinsky's tomb, with a bronze statue of the dancer in his costume for *Petroushka,* and the full-figure bronze by Jules Franceschi on the grave of Polish soldier Miecislas Kamienski, killed at the battle of Magenta in 1859.

Lapin Agile

Au Lapin Agile still operates nightly at 22, rue des Saules (**www.au-lapin-agile.com**). It doesn't serve food, but admission includes a drink and traditional *Montmartois* songs performed *a capella* by the resident singers.

Maintaining the local tradition, Place de Tertre is thronged by caricature artists, while musicians and other performers offer free entertainment on the steps and terrace in front of Sacré-Cœur, which offers a breathtaking panorama of the entire city.

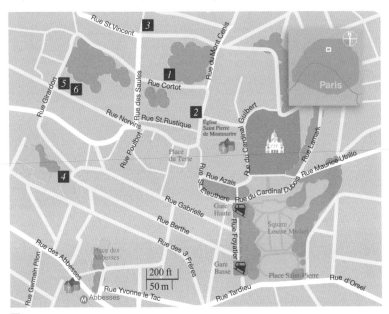

1 Musée de Montmartre: 12, rue Cortot
2 La Grande Artiste: 5, rue du Mont-Cenis
3 Lapin Agile: 22, rue des Saules
4 Bateau-Lavoir: 13, rue Ravignan (Place Emile Goudeau)
5 Marcel Ayme Apartment: Place Marcel Ayme
6 *The Walker-Through-Walls*

CHAPTER 18

ELLE EST PARTIE!

THE THEFT OF THE MONA LISA

On the morning of August 22, 1911, a person strolling along the Seine near the Musée du Louvre passed a man carrying a package wrapped in white cloth. As they crossed paths, the man tossed a shiny object into a ditch. The passer-by paused to look. He saw a well-rubbed metal doorknob. It was the first clue in the art theft of the century: the stealing of Leonardo da Vinci's masterpiece, the *Mona Lisa*.

Formerly the Paris residence of the royal family, the Louvre was the repository of a collection of art accumulated over centuries. Seized during the Revolution, it became a public gallery. Its 60,600 square meters (652,300 square feet) housed 35,000 objects, ranging from ancient Greek, Roman and Egyptian artifacts to the great paintings of the 19th century.

The theft was perfectly timed. Paris empties in August; even the director of the Louvre was on holiday. Also, the museum, as usual every Monday, was closed for maintenance. The only people moving through its vast galleries were workmen, dressed in the white smocks traditionally worn by painters. Some carried an artwork, perhaps for re-hanging or on its way to be photographed. So a plumber named Sauvet wasn't surprised, descending

‹ *Mona Lisa at the Louvre*, by Louis Béroud, 1911

Louis Béroud sketching the *Mona Lisa* in the Salon Carré, 1909

Vacant wall in the Salon Carré, Louvre, 1911

a staircase, to find a man in a smock, with a wrapped bundle, having trouble opening a door. The knob had come off in his hand—not uncommon in the ancient building. Sauvet used a pair of pliers to turn the bolt, and thought no more about it until the next morning, when panic swept the building. *La Joconde,* the masterpiece commonly known as the *Mona Lisa*, had disappeared. The Louvre's acting director, Georges Bénédite, broke the news. *"Elle est partie!"* he announced. She's gone.

A few months earlier, a 200-pound wooden case with a glass front had been built to enclose and protect the precious work. However, once the case was lifted off the four iron hooks that supported it and its elaborate frame was removed, the painting—though executed on a slab of poplar an inch and a half thick and weighing 18 pounds—was small enough to carry. The single guard on duty at the front door should have noticed the thief on his way out of the building, but he was fetching water to mop down the lobby, so the man simply walked out, pausing by the river to discard the doorknob, which, by coming off in his hand, furnished the sole glitch in a perfect theft.

The Louvre shut for a week as every corner of the museum was searched.

The police rounded up the usual suspects, including two foreigners with then-dubious reputations: Polish/Italian poet Guillaume Apollinaire and young Spanish painter Pablo Picasso. Apollinaire, a champion of new art, had urged, not very seriously, that the Louvre and its antique treasures be incinerated. Picasso seconded the motion. Moreover, the newspaper *Paris-Journal*, which offered a reward for information, told the police that a small-time conman, Honoré Pieret, had confessed that, while

Vincenzo Peruggia

working for Apollinaire, he'd stolen four antique Spanish stone heads from the Louvre, which Picasso bought. Picasso, "practically out of his mind with terror," according to his lover, Fernande Olivier, initially denied that he even knew Apollinaire, and finally convinced officials he wasn't involved in the *Mona Lisa* caper.

Police and customs instituted a thorough search. Any boat that sailed from the French port of Le Havre after the theft, particularly to the United States, was combed when it reached port. They found nothing—hardly surprising, since the painting never left Paris. The thief, Vincenzo Peruggia, a 30-year-old Italian carpenter at the Louvre, had helped to build the wooden case that protected it, which gave him time to hatch his plan. He entered the gallery on Sunday, when the museum was filled with tourists and amateur artists copying its masterpieces, and hid in the closet where these Sunday painters stored their tools. About 8 a.m. the next morning, wearing a painter's smock, he stepped out, just as the custodians started work. Having helped construct the case, he knew exactly how to lift it off the wall, take it apart, and remove the painting.

Once he got it out of the building, Peruggia hid *La Joconde* in his rented room, under the false bottom of a trunk. The police questioned him and searched his room as part of a check on everyone with access to the gallery at the time of the theft, but they failed to spot the painting. A single fingerprint was found on the case, but though Peruggia had been fingerprinted in an earlier run-in with the law, it was the practice at the time to print only the right hand, and the print found was from a left thumb.

Sauvet, the museum plumber, couldn't identify him either. "The light was too poor," he said, though surely he'd have remembered Peruggia's striking handlebar moustache.

When the *Mona Lisa* did resurface, 28 months later, it wasn't through diligent police work but because Peruggia got bored. He had quit his job at the Louvre and returned to Italy. There, he contacted Alfredo Geri, owner of an art gallery in Florence, and offered to surrender the painting. Giovanni Poggi, director of the Uffizi Gallery, informed the police. Upon his arrest, Peruggia said, "I am an Italian patriot that was seized by the desire to return to my Italy one of the numerous treasures that Napoleon stole from her." In fact, Napoleon was innocent. Leonardo gave the painting to France in gratitude for the patronage of Francois I. But the Italians were more than ready to believe the myth. Peruggia became a hero. Refusing to extradite him to France, the Italians gave him a few months in jail, while the *Mona Lisa* went on show in Florence and Rome to enormous crowds. As his reward for returning the painting, Geri asked for 10 percent of its value. The French refused, on the grounds that it was "beyond value," though he did receive a $5,000 reward and a decoration from the French government.

This might have ended the story, but for a 1932 article in *The Saturday Evening Post*. Journalist Karl Decker told of how, in 1914, in Morocco, he'd met Eduardo de Valfierno, a self-styled *marques* from Argentina. Valfierno boasted he had masterminded the *Mona Lisa* theft as part of an elaborate swindle. He claimed he'd hired a French forger named Yves Chaudron to make six copies of the painting. During the 28 months the whereabouts of the original were unknown, Valfierno sold these copies to gullible collectors for the equivalent of $67 million. Even better, he claimed, the copies were so good that the painting hanging in the Louvre was, in fact, one of Chaudron's fakes, while Peruggia still had the real one.

Was it true? Nobody ever verified Decker's story or the existence of Valfierno or Chaudron. And no copies have turned up. Peruggia, who returned to France and opened a paint store in Haut-Savoie, denied the whole thing. He died in 1947, silent to the last. And the *Mona Lisa*? Perhaps there is more than one secret behind that enigmatic smile.

THE ALLURE OF THE MONA LISA

Technically, the title of the *Mona Lisa* is *Portrait of Lisa Gherardini, wife of Francesco del Giocondo*. The common name of *La Gioconda* or, in French, *La Joconde*, meaning "the amused one," is a pun on her family name and her famous smile. Considered the most famous painting in the world, it is displayed in a room of the Salle des États, behind bulletproof glass, under climate-controlled conditions. Every year, some 6 million people visit the painting–though the average visitor spends a mere 15 seconds in front of it. Its value is incalculable, but was estimated in 2009 at $700 million.

One of the oddest traditions involving the Mona Lisa began with the suggestion that a trip to the Louvre is only complete if one has visited three works of art–the *Winged Victory of Samothrace*, the *Venus de Milo* and the *Mona Lisa*. After a satirical 1984 article by Art Buchwald about a supposed race to see these three items in the fastest time, a tradition was established known as "The Six Minute Louvre." Among the rules, the person must arrive and leave by taxi, circle the statue of Venus and pause before the *Winged Victory* and the *Mona Lisa* long enough to make an amusing comment. The record of six minutes was set by one Peter Stone, whose comment on the *Mona Lisa* was: "I know the man who has the original."

CHAPTER 19.

THE CORK-LINED ROOM
THE PAST TIME OF MARCEL PROUST

Few exhibits in the Musée Carnavalet attract more attention than the modest reconstruction of an early 20th century bedroom, its walls and ceiling covered in brown squares of cork. The narrow brass bed, the Chinese screen, the worn armchair, side table and bureau all came from the apartment of the writer Valentin Louis Georges Eugène Marcel Proust; the exhibit has the status of a shrine.

Between 1909 and his death in 1922, Proust worked in such a room, always at night, writing the seven novels of the cycle *À la Recherche du Temps Perdu*. First published in English as *Remembrance of Things Past*, it was later more accurately retitled *In Search of Lost Time*. The books minutely reconstruct the tangled lives of a few dozen fashionable Parisians as Proust observed them during his pampered upbringing and occasionally decadent early adulthood.

Many novelists wrote about the Belle Époque, but none with Proust's phenomenal sense memory. Stimulated by a taste, an odor or a few bars of music, he could summon up each detail of a room or a face not seen for decades. He discovered this ability when he nibbled a *madeleine*, a small fluted cake which he'd dunked in his tea. The combination of flavors triggered a rush of emotion, reminding him of how, on Sunday mornings during his sickly childhood in the village of Illiers, which he calls Combray, his aunt Léonie dipped a cake in her tea and offered him a few crumbs. He was overcome with a poignant sense of lost innocence.

The best-known portrait of Proust, by Jacques-Émile Blanche, was painted when he was 21. It shows an oval-faced, pale, tentative young man of fashion, with a neat moustache, deep-set eyes and a sensual, almost rosebud mouth. He wears an orchid in his buttonhole – unthinkable for someone racked as he was with bronchial asthma and multiple allergies, including one to flower pollen, but probably meant as a coded reference to his homosexuality. He would be one of the first authors to create openly gay characters, in particular the Baron de Charlus, a flamboyant aesthete who features in the fourth novel of *À la Recherche*, *Sodome et Gomorrhe*. Soon after the portrait was painted in 1892, Proust retreated indoors almost permanently, crippled by respiratory problems. The crude medicine of the time—"anti-asthma cigarettes" and powders that produced a pungent smoke—increased his pallor, as did his use of morphine. His moustache became thicker, his eyes deeper. He settled into the image by which he is best remembered; pensive, expressionless, chin resting on his hand, one finger raised skeptically against his cheek. If he did go out, it was at night, in a closed car, to dine at the Ritz Hotel. After his mother's death in 1905, he withdrew even further, protected by his fierce housekeeper, Celeste Albaret, and her husband Odilon, a former taxi driver who became his chauffeur.

Working all night on a board propped up on his knees, Proust filled thousands of pages with spidery writing. (In print, the cycle of novels runs to 4,200 pages.) He had the walls and ceiling lined with cork to mute the street noise. To stimulate his memory, he cluttered the room with his parents' furniture; his mother's grand piano, in particular, was a reminder of music's importance to the salons of the 1890s. "Music may be the unique example of what might have been the means of communicating between souls," he wrote.

Music carries particular significance for Charles Swann, a major character in the cycle. Already marginalized by his Jewishness and unfashionable political opinions, Swann marries Odette de Crécy, an expensive prostitute, and is ostracized by polite society. Still, he can't give her up. "To think that I have wasted years of my life, " he moans, "that I have longed for death, that the greatest love that I have ever known was for a woman who did not appeal to me, who was not my type!"

Sodome et Gomorrhe

What Swann called "the national anthem of their love" is a phrase from a string quartet by the composer he calls Venteuil, based on Cesar Franck's *String Quartet in D*. To remind himself of how it sounded, Proust summoned musicians to perform in his bedroom. They were happy to do so, even at 1 a.m., since the writer paid well. After the hour-long piece, he offered a snack of richly creamed mashed potatoes, fetched by Odilon from the Ritz. Then he asked them to play the whole quartet again. The cellist complimented him on the cork walls: "We've never sounded so good," he said. "Particularly not at three in the morning," the viola player added sourly.

All major presses rejected the first novel, *Du côté de chez Swann* (*Swann's Way*). One editor wrote "I just don't understand why a man should take thirty pages to describe how he rolls about in bed before he goes to sleep." Proust finally paid Grasset to publish it. The second volume, *À l'ombre des jeunes filles en fleurs* (*Within A Budding Grove*), didn't appear until 1919. By then, its achievement was obvious, even to former opponents like fellow novelist André Gide, who wrote Proust a letter of apology.

Proust survived bombing during World War I and was forced to leave the apartment in 1919 when his cousin sold the building to a bank. He died in 1922 at age 49 from an accidental overdose of adrenalin. The final volumes of his masterpiece appeared after his death and were universally hailed. His writing distills the essence of a society that didn't survive the Great War. Nobody who reads Proust's work can ever look at Paris—or the world—in the same way. This is just as he hoped. "The real voyage of discovery," he wrote, "consists not in seeking new lands but seeing with new eyes."

SEE IT: PROUST'S PARIS AND BEYOND

Proust's bedroom in the apartment at 102, boulevard Haussmann (1st *arrondissement*) where he wrote most of *À la Recherche du Temps Perdu*, is no longer open to the public, though the partial reconstruction in the Musée Carnavalet (3rd), with the real furniture, conveys some sense of his life. Otherwise, numerous sites on the right bank are associated with Proust.

As a child, he played in the Jardin des Champs-Élysées, a short walk from 9, boulevard Malesherbes (both 8th), the family home for 30 years. In these gardens, the narrator of the novels plays and falls in love with Charles Swann's daughter Gilberte. One path is now named Allée Marcel Proust. The buildings of two then-fashionable cabaret/cafés, Les Ambassadeurs and Alcazar d'Eté, survive as the Espace Pierre Cardin and Pavillon Gabriel, and the nearby Grand and Petit Palais exhibition halls have changed little since Proust's day.

In the 1st *arrondissement,* he frequently attended performances at the Opéra Garnier (Place de l'Opéra) and ate at the Ritz Hotel (15, place Vendôme). Angelina (226, rue de Rivoli), still serves the thick hot chocolate he liked. Jacques-Émile Blanche's portrait of Proust and Giovanni Boldini's of Count Robert de Montesquiou, a model for the Baron de Charlus, can both be found at the Musée d'Orsay.

The sites most evocative of Proust are not in central Paris. Fashionable society displayed itself on afternoons and weekends in the Bois de Boulogne, a wooded area of parks and riding trails at the edge of the 16th. (Though safe by day, the Bois should be avoided at night).

Proust spent part of his childhood in the village of Illiers, about an hour southwest by car or train. In 1971, it officially became Illiers-Combray. The house of Jules and Elisabeth Amiot (his "Tante Léonie") is now a museum, and one can walk to the Château de Villebon, which Proust called the Château de Guermantes, taking either "Swann's way" or "the Guermantes way" of the Duchess of Guermantes. While here, stop at the local pastry shops, which specialize in authentic *madeleines*.

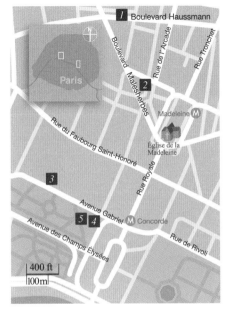

Map 1

1 Home of Marcel Proust:
102, boulevard Haussmann

2 Proust Family Home: 9, boulevard Malesherbes

3 Alcazar d'Eté: 5, avenue Gabriel

4 Les Ambassadeurs: 1-3, avenue Gabriel

5 Jardin des Champs-Élysées/Alée Marcel Proust

Map 2

6 Musée Carnavalet: 23, rue de Sévigné

CHAPTER 20

"LAFAYETTE, WE ARE HERE!"

AMERICA AND FRANCE IN WORLD WAR I

In August 1914, Germany attacked France through southern Belgium, aiming to seize Paris and overpower the country in a few days. With an emergency injection of British help, the French army managed to halt the invaders along the River Marne, only 43 miles from Paris—so close that, in September 1914, 4,000 reinforcements were rushed to the front in a fleet of taxis.

Each side dug in. Despite artillery barrages, mustard gas attacks and repeated offensives aimed at ending the stalemate, little would change over the next three years along the 400 miles of trenches, reaching from the Belgian border to the Swiss frontier, that made up Germany's Western Front. The war news in German newspapers almost invariably announced *"Im Westen nichts Neues"* (*"Nothing new in the West"*). The phrase became famous when Erich Maria Remarque used it in 1929 as the title of his best-selling novel, *All Quiet on the Western Front*.

Parisians also did their best to act as if nothing unusual was taking place. After a period of curfew, the military authorities, realizing invasion was no longer imminent, permitted cafés to re-open and allowed people back

General John J. Pershing leading a parade of the First Division, American Expeditionary Force, 1919

on the streets after dark. Prostitutes once again cruised Montmartre and Montparnasse. Music halls added patriotic numbers to their programs, sometimes with hilarious effect; British "Tommies" on leave roared with laughter to see their brisk marching song *Tipperary* performed as a tragic ballad, with the singer, shot by a German firing squad, croaking "Goodbye, Piccadilly. Farewell, Leicester Square," with her last breath.

Magazines like the "naughty" weekly *La Vie Parisienne* also went on a war footing, featuring centerfolds of pretty Parisiennes consorting with young lieutenants on leave. *Regiment*, filled with saucy cartoons, was published specifically for officers, while *La Baionnette* (*The Bayonet*) targeted *poilus*, or enlisted men. Its cartoons showed fat, cowardly Germans in retreat or benign angels spreading protective arms over the Allied trenches. Neither obscured the reality of what was happening just over the horizon. That was illustrated by the amputees and other walking wounded who hobbled along the streets or sat with haunted faces over their cognac in cafés.

French magazine celebrating the English soldiers ("Tommies") and Scots servicement ("Jocks").

Magazines such as *Regiment* reminded officers at the front of the pleasures awaiting them behind the lines.

Though the United States remained neutral, many Americans were eager to get into the war. In 1914, expatriates in Paris tried to form an American Volunteer Force. Its first recruits were students who had relied on regular payments sent from home for living expenses. With currency transfers suspended, they had to fend for themselves. Signing up for military service at least guaranteed them meals. Other expatriates took more direct action. In September 1914, 60 young Chinese invaded their embassy and emptied the ambassadorial kitchen.

The French had no desire for independent fighting units commanded by foreign nationals, particularly self-styled soldiers of the kind who hung around Paris. If Americans wanted to help, it was suggested, they could join the Foreign Legion. Since this no-questions-asked unit, a refuge for fugitives and troublemakers, was customarily posted to the worst hellholes of France's Asian and African colonies, the prospect was uninviting. Instead, American writers and intellectuals, including Ernest Hemingway, Dashiell Hammett, E.E. Cummings and John Dos Passos, volunteered to become non-combatant ambulance drivers.

Pilots were more rare and more valuable than infantry, so the French and British accepted American fliers as early as 1916, though always under

Allied command. Many flew with the Lafayette Escadrille and Lafayette Flying Corps, named for the Marquis de Lafayette, who fought with George Washington during the American War of Independence. Once the United States entered the war, the 94th Aero Squadron, famous for its "Hat in the Ring"

General Pershing at the grave of Lafayette, 1917

emblem, joined the fight. Pilots like Eddie Rickenbacker helped it rack up a record 60 kills.

Although it had long supplied the Allies with arms and equipment, the United States only officially entered the conflict in April 1917. The first troops of the American Expeditionary Force landed in France in June, commanded by General John J. "Black Jack" Pershing. On July 4, he marched through Paris at the head of his troops to the grave of Lafayette. As he saluted the tomb, his aide, Colonel Charles E. Stanton, announced, "Lafayette, we are here!"

After this, life for the Americans settled down to training and negotiation. Since most troops had arrived without their own artillery or transport, the A.E.F. didn't see action until October 1917. Pershing, a last-minute replacement for the mission when the original candidate died, was a theorist who, famously, "led from the rear," plotting his tactics from command headquarters and employing rules of combat that dated back to before Napoleon.

The French made sure that the wait, at least for the high command, was painless. A committee of aristocrats, recognizing that good food and wine were essential to any meeting of minds, set up the Cercle de l'Union Interalliée, a private social and dining club in the most fashionable area of

Paris on the rue Fauboug-Saint-Honoré. There commanders like Marshal Philippe Pétain could entertain foreign colleagues such as Pershing. Its president was the Supreme Commander of the Allied Armies, Marshal Ferdinand Foch.

Regular soldiers, called "doughboys" because of their dusty grey/brown uniforms, didn't suffer either. Though donors back home sent thousands of books and magazines, few servicemen were interested in curling up with a novel. Bars and brothels did a roaring trade. The freethinking, free-drinking, sexually liberated culture of France left an indelible mark. Songs like *How Ya Gonna Keep 'em Down On the Farm (After They've Seen Paree?)* dramatized the ways the collision of U.S. servicemen and the French capital changed one another.

African-American soldiers in particular relished the French indifference to race, which contrasted with the discrimination within their own command. Some black troops did see action, in particular the 369th Infantry Regiment, known as the Harlem Hellfighters, but most were employed as laborers. After the war, a number joined the migration of writers and artists that fertilized the rich period of expatriate literature during the so-called *années folles* or "crazy years" of the 1920s. Most found jobs in the *Bars Americaines* that proliferated, as tourists flooding into Paris demanded the martinis, Manhattans and Old Fashioneds that the French never drank. A black American barman became *de rigeur* in every large café, along with a jazz band of African-American musicians.

The soldiers continued to bide their time as Pershing waited for the moment to attack. The general considered the trench system a strategy of weakness and insisted that superior American marksmanship and spirit would prevail once his troops could attack in strength. Until then, he refused to let his men be sent as replacements to British or French units. His belief proved disastrously wrong once the Allies launched their final offensive in the winter of 1918. Waves of American infantry, sent into battle with minimal artillery support, sustained huge losses, particularly in the Meuse-Argonne assault, the bloodiest single battle in U.S. military history. To divert attention from this debacle, the army played up the feat of Sergeant Alvin York, who, on October 8 1918, captured 32 machine guns, killed 28 Germans and captured 132 more. A god-fearing sharpshooter from Tennessee, he exemplified Pershing's image of the ideal American soldier and was awarded the Congressional Medal of Honor. In 1941, the film *Sergeant York,* based vaguely on York's life and starring Gary Cooper, encouraged Americans to enlist in World War II.

The United States would lose 116,708 servicemen and women in World War I, more than a quarter of them from accidents and disease. Twenty-five thousand alone died in the influenza pandemic of 1918. Despite such loses, Pershing was celebrated on both sides of the Atlantic. In France, the YMCA built Pershing Stadium on land in the Parc de Vincennes donated by the government; during June and July 1919, it was the site of the Inter-Allied Games. Serving and former military personnel from 18 countries took part; medal winners included future world heavyweight boxing champion Gene Tunney.

Back in the United States, Pershing was made Chief of Staff of the Army, and was even asked to consider running for president. Years later, in July 1944, he was visited by Charles de Gaulle, leader of the Free French forces. Pershing, whose memory had deteriorated, asked after his old colleague, Philippe Pétain. De Gaulle replied, diplomatically, that, last time he saw him, he had looked well. He didn't mention that Petain was his greatest enemy, having turned his coat and become head of the puppet Vichy government, controlled by the occupying Germans.

SEE IT: REMNANTS OF WAR

Most World War I military cemeteries are on the battlefields of the Marne and the Somme. The closest to Paris is the Suresnes American Cemetery and Memorial. The 7.5-acre site holds the remains of 1,541 Americans who died in World War I and 24 unknown dead of World War II. The Marquis de Lafayette is buried in the Cimetière de Picpus (35, rue Picpus, 12th *arrondissement*), where an American flag flies over the grave at all times.

The books sent to American soldiers became the basis of the American Library in Paris (10, rue General Camou, 7th), the only English-language circulating library in the city. The Cercle de l'Union Interalliée (33, rue du Faubourg Saint-Honoré, 8th), the club where generals once met, flourished after the war. Because of its lavish décor and proximity to the British, American and Japanese embassies, it is a popular venue for prestigious receptions. Reciprocal privileges are extended to many American groups, including the Army Navy Club of Washington, D.C., and the Harvard Club of Boston.

Other reminders of the American presence in Paris include the mural in the departure hall at the Gare de l'Est, presented to the nation by American artist Albert Herter in 1925. It shows French soldiers departing for the front in 1914. Herter's son Everit, a camouflage artist, was killed in 1918. The Stade Pershing closed in 1960, but has been refurbished and reopened as a center for baseball and softball.

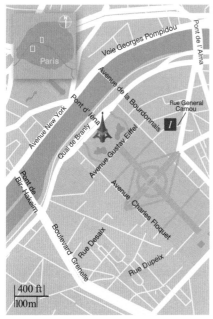

Map 1

1 American Library: 10, rue General Camou

Map 2

2 Cercle de l'Union Interalliée: 33, rue du Faubourg Saint-Honoré

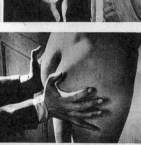
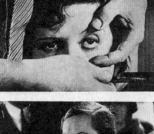

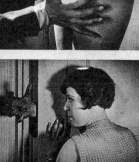

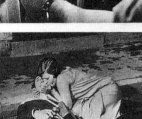

UN CHIEN ANDALOU

UN FILM DE LUIS BUÑUEL ET SALVADOR DALÍ

CHAPTER 21

SHOOTING INTO THE CROWD

SURREALISM

"The simplest Surrealist act," wrote André Breton, founder of Surrealism, "consists of dashing down into the street, pistol in hand and firing blindly, as fast as you can pull the trigger, into the crowd."

Founded in Paris in the early 1920s, Surrealism is the art of the absurd — a philosophy that transcended its original form, writing, and reached into painting, film and even into the daily lives of its practitioners. Though no Surrealist is known to have taken a gun into the street, at the height of anti-Teutonic sentiment after World War I, the poet Benjamin Péret appeared at a busy Paris café in the uniform of a German soldier, which almost caused a riot. He also acted on the movement's dislike of religion, attacking nuns and priests in the street.

Breton periodically led the group in attacks on dramatists of whom they disapproved, such as Jean Cocteau, and performers like the German dancer Valeska Gert who falsely claimed to be "Surrealist." After disrupting performances and sometimes wrecking theaters and galleries, Breton sent a letter of apology to the management — adding a spot of blood on the corner of the paper, a warning that he meant business.

< *Un Chien Andalou*, (or *An Andalusian Dog*), a film directed by Luis Buñel and Salvador Dalí, 1929

André Breton

Brasserie Cyrano, c. 1920

At the turn of the century, Sigmund Freud popularized the belief that we reveal our true selves in dreams, but artists had been experimenting with this idea for a century. In France, Charles Baudelaire and Isidore Lucien Ducasse, the Comte de Lautréamont, wrote under the influence of drugs, hallucination or insanity. The images they created held a mysterious appeal; Lautréamont, for instance, described a boy as being as "beautiful as the chance meeting on a dissecting-table of a sewing-machine and an umbrella."

During World War I, Tristan Tzara created Dada, a movement that celebrated spontaneity: his *Dada Manifesto* of 1918 began "Dada does not mean anything!" Its techniques included creating poems by randomly drawing words from a hat. James Joyce was impressed. So was André Breton, a medical assistant in a French hospital. He had become fascinated with the fantasies of shell-shocked soldiers, and encouraged his patients to write down their dreams. The result proved, he claimed, that the greatest art was "dictated by thought, without any control exercised by reason, and exempt from any aesthetic or moral concern."

Breton moved to Paris in 1918 and co-founded the magazine *Littérature* with two young poets, Louis Aragon and Philippe Soupault. He and Soupault adapted Dada methods to pioneer "automatic writing": recording random thoughts without any concern for logic or form. Their texts, published as *Les Champs Magnétiques (The Magnetic Fields)*, attracted young and adventurous writers like Paul Éluard, René Crevel, Michel Leiris, Benjamin Péret, Antonin Artaud and Robert Desnos. The movement was named by Guillaume Apollinaire, who called their work "*surrealiste*" or "above realism." In 1924, Breton published the first *Surrealist Manifesto*.

"The marvellous is always beautiful," it announced. "Anything marvellous is beautiful; in fact *only* the marvellous is beautiful."

Breton didn't look like a revolutionary. The son of a provincial policeman, he smoked a pipe and wore green tweed suits, with collar and tie. Despite his adulation of the erotic, he disapproved of homosexuality (although Surrealist writer René Crevel was gay), and frowned on members spending time in brothels or in the cafés of bohemian Montparnasse. He also insisted that no Surrealist write for a living; paid work wasn't spontaneous. Less wealthy members resigned rather than starve, and still others left when he ordered everyone to join the Communist party.

Breton spent his days working in his apartment on Place Blanche in Montmartre. At 7:30 p.m., he crossed to the Brasserie Cyrano for a meeting of the group, known as a *séance*. Attendance was obligatory. The only legitimate excuse for absence was that you had been making love; sex, a primal urge, was out of one's control. Sometimes he simply held forth, while his followers listened in respectful silence. On other occasions, new works were presented. In 1930, Salvador Dalí previewed his latest "object," a dinner jacket hung with whisky glasses full of milk. Aragon, a radical Communist, attacked him for wasting milk in a world where children were starving, and the meeting dissolved in furious argument.

In lighter moments, the group invoked chance with games like *Cadavre Exquis* (Exquisite Corpse), in which each person added a phrase to a sentence, without looking at what went before. The name came from an early success: "The exquisite corpse will drink the young wine." At the core of the group's philosophy was the idea that any action could be Surrealist, providing it was unplanned. Writer George Melly enlivened a restaurant *séance* of the London Surrealists by gathering up all the cutlery at table and flinging it into the air. After the group was thrown out, he occupied a phone booth, rang people at random and shouted part of a poem by the artist Jean Arp: "The stones are full of guts! Hurrah!"

Artists from all over the world, hearing of Surrealism, gravitated to Paris in the '20s. As well as Dalí and his filmmaker collaborator Luis Buñuel from Spain, photographer Man Ray came from the United States, painters Max Ernst from Germany and René Magritte from Belgium. Breton welcomed

Salvador Dalí and Man Ray, Paris, 1934

them all, not realizing that, in admitting visual artists, he was forcing out the writers with whom he founded the movement, and, in the process, making his own role obsolete.

With painters replacing poets, everything changed. Poetry had only a small audience but everyone recognized Magritte's paintings of rocks floating weightless as balloons and faces with the features replaced by breasts, a navel and pubic hair. Nor could anyone forget *Un Chien Andalou (An Andalusian Dog)*, the film by Dalí and Buñuel with its notorious scene of a woman's eyeball slashed by a razor. Dalí, a genius at self-promotion, was soon proclaiming, "I am Surrealism." He moved to the United States, worked in Hollywood for Alfred Hitchcock and Walt Disney, and even appeared on the cover of *Time* magazine. Back in Paris, Breton twisted his name into the contemptuous anagram "Avida Dollars," hungry for money.

Breton lived until 1966, watching Surrealism become increasingly debased by Dalí and rejected by art historians as outdated. In the '60s, he complained to Buñuel, "It's impossible to shock people any more." Yet it was exactly when Surrealism could no longer shock that interest revived and today,

although the work of its writers, including Breton, remain obscure, few styles in painting and sculpture are more recognized and discussed.

The absurdist in Breton may have taken some cold consolation in that.

Dali atomicus, Salvador Dali, c. 1948

SEE IT: THE SURREAL SIDE OF PARIS

In his novel *Nadja*, Breton writes: "My point of departure will be the Hôtel des Grandes Hommes, Place du Pantheon, where I lived in 1918." It was here that he and Philippe Soupault made their experiments in automatic writing. A plaque on the front of the hotel (5th *arrondissement*) commemorates the event. A plaque also appears in the portico of the Hôtel Delambre on 35, rue Delambre (14th), where Breton lived in 1921. Disgusted by the idle life of Montparnasse, he moved to 42, rue Fontaine in working-class Montmartre (9th) where he remained for the rest of his life. Breton's disapproval of Montparnasse didn't discourage Man Ray, who lived and worked at 31, rue Campagne-Première in the 14th. Next door, the historic Hôtel Istria boasts a large plaque listing the writers and artists, many of them Surrealists, who visited.

Plaque at Hôtel Delambre

In his novel, Breton encounters the mysterious Nadja on Place Dauphine (1st), a secluded triangle behind the Palais de Justice. Because of its suggestive shape, he described it as *"le sexe de Paris,"* and endowed it with an air of mystery.

Studio 28

The Brasserie Cyrano, which hosted Surrealist *séances*, no longer exists; neither does Breton's original apartment. Attempts to preserve it as a museum failed and his huge collection was sold at auction in 2003. Other important Surrealist sites include the small independent cinema Studio 28 (10, rue Tholoze, 18th). In 1930, right-wing rowdies wrecked it during a screening of the Dalí/Buñuel film *L'age d'or*, which was subsequently banned and withdrawn from circulation for many years. A small exhibition in the lobby includes photographs of the event.

The best collection of Surrealist art in Paris is held in the Centre Pompidou. Along with canvases by Ernst, Dalí, De Chirico, Tanguy and many others, the museum showcases one wall of Breton's apartment, with a representative selection of his holdings.

CHAPTER 22

COCO CHANEL
LITTLE BLACK DRESSMAKER

"Fashion is not something that exists in dresses only," Gabrielle Bonheur "Coco" Chanel once said. "Fashion is in the sky, in the street; fashion has to do with ideas, the way we live, what is happening." Audacious, inventive, cunning, she lived just one step ahead of the heavy tread of history, always managing at the last minute to scurry out from under its crushing feet.

Learning survival came early. Her washerwoman mother died of tuberculosis in 1895 when Chanel was just 12, her market trader father disappeared, and young Coco spent the next six years in the convent at Aubazine, in central France, learning a useful trade—dressmaking. The techniques she learned there—plain sewing of basic materials and simple styles—became the foundation of her success as a *couturière,* since it was there she developed her famous suits and "little black dresses."

As a teenager, Chanel gravitated to the larger town of Moulins, where she scandalized relatives by singing in bars for officers from the nearby cavalry school. A mediocre *chanteuse* and not particularly pretty, she compensated by being bold. Various officers made her their mistress, nicknaming her "Coco"; short for "*coquette*" (a flirt) or "*coquine*" (naughty); nobody is sure.

One of her cavalry lovers, Étienne Balsan, heir to a textile fortune, set her up as a dressmaker and introduced her to high society. When she moved to Paris in 1909, she took over his apartment, even though she had a new lover—the wealthy, polo-playing Englishman Arthur Edward Capel, known, because of his youthful good looks, as "Boy."

Capel paid to launch Chanel in a chain of boutiques, starting with one in Deauville, the fashionable resort on the Channel coast. Looking for an entry into the competitive fashion market, Chanel had begun by designing hats. Her first creations were explosions of plumes and veils, but she quickly moved on, remarking: "How can a brain function under those things?" Instead, she adapted the berets, felts and soft straws worn by her neighbors in Aubazine. They were an instant success.

Chanel hoped to marry Capel, but propriety demanded he take a wife from the British aristocracy. Even after marriage, he continued to see her in Paris. His car crash death in 1919 devastated her, and she had a monument erected by the road where he was killed. The relationship's legacy was Chanel's introduction to British society, including the Duke of Westminster, the richest man in England, who, from 1925 to 1930, became her lover. Through him, she met public figures like Winston Churchill, a useful friend. More importantly, Capel introduced Chanel to British tailoring. Traditionally, tweed was used for hunting outfits, but Chanel adapted it to women's suits, which she lined with her trademark: quilted silk. Small gold chains sewn into the hems ensured they hung perfectly. The houndstooth fabric pattern known as "Prince of Wales" became a Chanel specialty. At a time when women wore tight corseted silhouettes, Chanel made dresses from soft wool jersey, used until then for winter underwear, and turned the flannel blazer worn by English schoolboys and cricketers into a jacket for women.

In 1921, she launched a perfume, Chanel No. 5. There was no No. 1, 2, 3 or 4. Given the choice of five fragrances, she chose the fifth. But her skill in presentation was even stronger than her sense of smell. At her suggestion, the square bottle imitated the dimensions of Place Vendôme, Paris's most chic square, famous for its jewelers. In 1924, she licensed the fragrance to the Wertheimer family. Not anticipating its remarkable success, she accepted a mere 10 percent of the profits—a deal she fought for 20 years to overturn.

Couturier Coco Chanel with Surrealist artist Salvador Dalí

Her "little black dress" of 1926 became her trademark, the epitome of discreet but distinctive taste. "My art," she said, "has consisted in cutting off what others added." Such light, simple clothing perfectly suited the Riviera. When she stepped off the Duke of Westminster's yacht in 1923 with a heavy tan, the whole Côte d'Azur got a touch of the sun. "I think she may have invented sunbathing," said Prince Jean-Louis de Faucigny-Lucinge. "At that time, she invented everything."

Chanel and show business were natural allies. She was friendly with ballet impresario Serge Diaghilev and had an affair with Igor Stravinsky, his star composer. In 1924, she designed costumes for *Le Train Bleu,* a ballet named for the express that brought holidaymakers to the Côte d'Azur. Producer Samuel Goldwyn invited her to Hollywood in 1931, but though she designed clothes for Katharine Hepburn and, much later, Grace Kelly, she wearied of California. In 1934, she returned to Paris and her headquarters at 31, rue

☐
M

Coco Chanel in her hotel suite

Cambon, which included a street-level boutique, fitting rooms, a top-floor design studio, and a three-room private apartment, linked by a mirrored spiral staircase—always scented with Chanel No. 5—where she sat during her shows, able watch the audience without being seen. At the same time, she took a suite at the Ritz Hotel, almost next door, where she lived for the rest of her life.

Under Nazi occupation, Chanel closed her boutiques and shared her bed at the Ritz with her German lover Hans Günther von Dincklage, who supervised the French textile industry. Mindful of her contacts with Churchill and the British aristocracy, the Germans gave her privileged status, and she is rumored to have visited England secretly as part of a possible peace initiative. Meanwhile, Chanel, constantly reminded of Chanel No. 5 by the view from her bedroom window of Place Vendôme, tried to claw back control from the Wertheimers under the Nazi's Jewish confiscation rules.

In 1945, she was arrested as a collaborator but was released, supposedly on Churchill's orders. She fled to Switzerland. A new deal with the Wertheimers in 1947 made her one of the world's richest women. She could have continued in comfortable exile, but the post-war revival in fashion with the "New Look" drew her back to Paris, and she was soon again queen of couture. She was overseeing her 1971 spring collection, when, at 87, she died—in style to the end—in her suite at the Ritz.

CHANEL IN PARIS

Unless one counts the various boutiques, there are few Chanel sites around Paris. Though her rue Cambon apartment is not open to the public, virtual visits are offered by various websites. If money is no object, visitors can pay $4,300 a night to occupy her suite at the Ritz, its decor recreated

Ritz Hotel

by Karl Lagerfeld, who inherited control of the brand. The hotel overlooks Place Vendôme, which remains as splendid now as when it inspired the bottle of Chanel No. 5, which, of course, you can buy for nearly $200 for half an ounce.

For a less pricey taste of Chanel's Paris, visit Café Angelina on rue de Rivoli, where many fashionable people, including Chanel, took tea or chocolate; the café has not lost any of its chic. Examples of the designer's iconic creations are held in the Museum of Fashion & Textiles, located at 107, rue de Rivoli (1st *arrondissement*) and the Musée de la Mode et du Costume de la Ville de Paris, Palais Galliéra, 10, avenue Pierre-1er-de-Serbie (16th).

Some travel companies offer three-day tours of the towns where she grew up, including Aubazine, Saumur, in the Loire Valley and Deauville, the English Channel resort where she opened her first boutique in 1913.

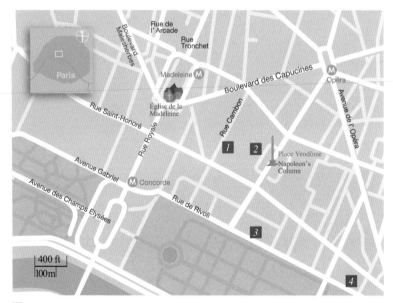

1 Chanel Boutique & Apartment: 33, rue Cambon
2 Ritz Paris: 15, place Vendôme
3 Café Angelina: 226, rue de Rivoli
4 Museum of Fashion and Textiles: 107, rue de Rivoli

PHOTOGRAPH OF B

No. 359666

CHAPTER 23.

THE IMPORTANCE OF BEING ERNEST

HEMINGWAY IN PARIS

Ernest Hemingway is the classic expatriate. Nobody did more to create the archetype of the writer abroad, seeking new experiences to inspire original fiction. Until the 1920s, for an artist to flee his country represented a betrayal. As his character Bill Gorton sneers to Hemingway's hero Jake Barnes in *The Sun Also Rises*, "You're an expatriate. You've lost touch with the soil. You get precious. Fake European standards have ruined you. You drink yourself to death. You become obsessed by sex. You spend all your time talking, not working. You are an expatriate, see? You hang around cafés."

Hemingway made it not only permissible to be an expatriate but honorable. He came to Paris before the United States entered World War I, volunteered as an ambulance driver for the Italian army and was wounded and hospitalized. In 1922, he moved to Paris with his first wife, Hadley Richardson, and wrote *A Farewell to Arms* about his tragic love affair with a nurse during his convalescence. His clipped writing, free of adjectives, suggested a man as hard-boiled as his prose—an image Hemingway, actually clumsy, sensitive and romantic, struggled all his life to maintain. He drank heavily and pursued aggressive sports like boxing and big-game hunting, for which he had no talent. In a famous encounter, he was knocked down repeatedly by Canadian writer Morley Callaghan, who was shorter and lighter, but a more skilled boxer. Hemingway also cultivated an interest in bull-fighting and reported on war from dangerously close to the front line. These activities left him a physical and emotional wreck.

American publishers initially spurned his short stories as plotless and bleak. They first appeared from small Paris publishers like Robert McAlmon's Contact Press, and in the magazine *transition*. Until the success of *A Farewell to Arms*, he survived mainly on articles in provincial U.S. papers. Many were written in Montparnasse cafés, where he was sustained by a succession of coffees and cheap cognacs. So inexpensive was Paris in those days that, as he wrote in a 1922 article, one could live there on $1,000 a year.

His 1924 novel *The Sun Also Rises,* his first success, glamorized and satirised the expatriates Gertrude Stein called "The Lost Generation." Its hero, Jake Barnes, castrated by a war wound, is hopelessly in love with promiscuous Lady Brett Ashley. Most saw Barnes as a surrogate Hemingway, better able to adore women than relate to them. His picture of the hard-drinking loafers who hung around Montparnasse, making an occasional excursion to Pamplona in Spain for the running of the bulls, included a number of recognizable caricatures, among them humorist Donald Ogden Stewart as Bill Gorton and magazine editor Harold Loeb as Robert Cohn.

Paris remained the city where Hemingway felt most at home. He believed it had a special capacity to inspire creativity and to enhance the quality of life. His memoir of those years, published posthumously as *A*

^ Pamplona, Spain, summer 1926. Left to right at table: Gerald Murphy, Sara Murphy, Pauline Pfeiffer, Ernest Hemingway and Hadley Hemingway.

Ernest Hemingway with Sylvia Beach (second from right) and her staff in front of Shakespeare and Company.

Moveable Feast, though heavily fictionalized, is one of his best-loved works. Only in the woods and streams of Michigan, depicted in the stories *Up in Michigan* and *Big Two-Hearted River,* did he achieve the same vividness of description.

The cafés of Montparnasse, were, for him, as much places of work as of recreation. After a day spent writing in his rented room or in the Closerie des Lilas, he would meet friends at the Dingo Bar or the Dôme, gathering material for more stories. When inspiration failed, he dropped in on Sylvia Beach at Shakespeare and Company to borrow books from her lending library or ate at Brasserie Lipp—almost always the same meal; *cervelas* sausage with cold potatoes and a beer. Until they fell out, he was also a regular guest at the weekly salons of Gertrude Stein and her companion Alice B. Toklas.

In *A Moveable Feast,* Hemingway is unsparing with those who, through what he sees as character faults or a failure of courage, didn't take full

John "Bumby" Hemingway and
Gertrude Stein. Paris, 1924

Scott and Zelda Fitzgerald with daughter
Scottie at their apartment in Paris, 1921

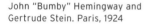

advantage of Paris's opportunities. In particular F. Scott Fitzgerald, one
of his closest friends, appears as weak, alcoholic and dominated by his
mentally disturbed wife Zelda. He also scorned Fitzgerald's adulation of
wealthier expatriates like Gerald and Sara Murphy, the inspiration of his
novel *Tender is the Night*. This hostility inspired a famous, though possibly
apocryphal, exchange. Fitzgerald told Hemingway "The rich are very
different to you and I, Ernest." Hemingway responded sourly, "Yes, they
have more money."

Hemingway left Paris in 1928 and spent the rest of his life a wanderer. In the
1930s, he involved himself in the Spanish Civil War, as journalist and fund-
raiser for the Anti-Fascists. He drew upon the experience to write the novel
For Whom the Bell Tolls. Living in Cuba at the outbreak of World War II, he
formed a private navy and intelligence service of fellow expatriates. Called
the Crook Factory, it armed a cabin cruiser to hunt German submarines, of
which it found none.

The U.S. Army reluctantly allowed Hemingway back into France after D-Day. He led a piratical platoon of journalists and cameramen well in advance of the Allied forces and, defying the rules governing non-combatant war correspondents, attacked and killed fleeing Germans. After "liberating" Shakespeare and Company, he installed himself in a suite at the Ritz, next to fellow correspondent (and later, wife) Mary Welsh. Too poor before the war to drink there, he made the hotel his post-war headquarters, inventing a potent martini, the Montgomery. Its 17 parts gin to one part vermouth reflected, Hemingway said, the superiority over the enemy demanded by his *bête noire,* British Field Marshal Montgomery, before he went into battle; 17 of his men to one German.

For Whom the Bell Tolls

Hemingway's post-war writing varied in quality, but his novella *The Old Man and the Sea*, a major best-seller, did much to earn him a 1954 Nobel Prize. He continued to drink heavily, and safaris to Africa twice concluded in near-fatal plane crashes. He returned to his home state of Idaho, suffering from bipolar disorder, alcohol dependence, traumatic brain injury and probable borderline and narcissistic personality traits. In 1961, he committed suicide, using the same shotgun with which his father killed himself.

After Hemingway's death, the text for *A Moveable Feast* was supposedly found in a trunk left in the basement of the Ritz. The accuracy of the episodes is questionable, but the city they reflect has established itself in legend. Stein gave the name to "The Lost Generation" but Hemingway made it, and Paris, immortal.

SEE IT: HEMINWAY IN PARIS

Closephoto des Lilas

Le Dingo Bar

Many remnants of Hemingway's Paris survive. On the right bank, the Ritz Hotel (15 place Vendôme, 1st *arrondissement*) maintains a shrine-like Hemingway Bar, though he never actually drank there. In his time, it was the ladies' bar—women being banned from the main bar. Brasserie Lipp (151, boulevard Saint-Germain, 6th) still serves his favourite *cervelas* sausage and potato salad. A brass plate marks his favourite table at the Closerie des Lilas (171, boulevard de Montparnasse, 6th), and there is a plaque on the building at 74, rue du Cardinal-Lemoine (5th) where he lived for a time.

Hemingway and Fitzgerald first met at the former Dingo Bar on rue Delambre, behind La Coupole, now the Auberge de Venise (10, rue Delambre, 14th). When he first came to Paris, he stayed at the Hôtel d'Angleterre (44, rue Jacob, 6th), which maintains a small display about him in the lobby. When he left Hadley to live with Pauline Pfeiffer, they had an apartment at 6 bis, rue Ferou (6th).

Seeking inspiration in all corners of the city, Hemingway often visited the nearby Musée de Luxembourg, which housed the national collection of Cézannes, the artist whose style he hoped to mirror in his prose. He attended parties at the home of Gertrude Stein and Alice B. Toklas, (27, rue de Fleurus, 6th). The original Shakespeare and Company bookshop was at 12, rue de l'Odéon (6th) and the home of Sylvia Beach at No. 18.

Ernest Hemingway outside of his residence at 13, rue Notre-Dame-des-Champs, Paris, c. 1924

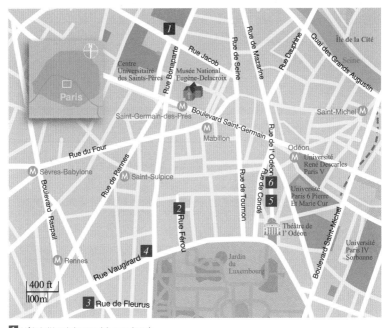

1 Hôtel d'Angleterre: 44, rue Jacob
2 Home of Ernest Hemmingway: 6 bis, rue Férou
3 Home of Gertrude Stein: 27, rue de Fleurus
4 Home of Zelda and Scott Fitzgerald: 58, rue Vaugirard
5 Home of Sylvia Beach and Adrienne Monnier: 18, rue de l'Odéon
6 Shakespeare and Company (1921-1944): 12, rue de l'Odéon

CHAPTER 24.

THE SADNESS OF ST. LOUIS
DJANGO REINHARDT AND
LE JAZZ HOT

Everyone knew the guitarist Jean-Baptiste Reinhardt by his nickname Django—"I'm awake" in the Romani gypsy dialect. But when, for his first record, he was asked how he spelt it, he had no idea, since he could neither read or write. The producer shrugged and made a guess with "Jiango Renard."

Through the first half of the 20th century, white audiences liked to think that African-American, gypsy or Hispanic musicians were musically illiterate. Such performers were valued for spontaneity and improvisational skill. Many, of course, were highly educated in music. The first U.S. military band to arrive in France in 1917 consisted entirely of African-Americans, led by James Reese Europe, former musical director for the dancers Vernon and Irene Castle. All could read music, but they never did so in public.

Django Reinhardt reinforced the image of the player with "a natural sense of rhythm." Born in Belgium in 1910, he was entirely self-taught, although his father, who'd long since abandoned the family, was a professional player of violin, cimbalom, guitar and piano, and the leader of a touring *orchestre tzigane* before the First World War. As a boy, Django astonished

Django Reinhardt and his Nouveau Quintet

everyone with his skill on guitar, banjo and violin. An accordionist once bet he couldn't replay from memory the 17 tunes a band had just performed. Not only did Reinhardt do so, and in the correct order, but on a banjo too large for his young fingers, and using, instead of a flexible plectrum, a whalebone collar stiffener.

Like most Romani, his family traveled around France and Belgium, selling handicrafts they made themselves: cane furniture, artificial flowers and wooden toys. When not playing, Django carved delicate models of the caravans in which they lived. In 1928, returning home late and drunk, he tipped a candle into some celluloid flowers. The fire consumed the caravan and almost killed him. His left side was badly burned. Thereafter, he walked with a limp, often using a cane.

Worse, he lost the use of two fingers on his left hand. Unable any longer to finger the violin, he retrained himself to play the guitar, using his two functioning fingers to make chords. It created a light, fast style suited to American jazz. After World War I, jazz took root in France, as many African-American soldiers, weary of discrimination at home, refused repatriation and instead found work in clubs and cafés as barmen or musicians.

With alcohol prohibited in the United States, tourists flocked to Paris, which acquired a reputation both for unlimited drinking and what the French called *le jazz hot*. Enterprising café owners in the area of Saint-Germain-des-Prés turned their cellars, normally used for storage, into jazz venues, creating the cliché of the congested, smoke-filled basement club with a sweating trio crowded onto a tiny bandstand.

Jamming backstage at the Hôtel Claridge in Paris, Reinhardt and his brother Joseph, also a guitarist, met violinist Stéphane Grappelli and bassist Louis Vola. They blended so perfectly that an association of critics and writers led by Charles Delaunay and Hugues Panassié, devoted to jazz appreciation, underwrote some concerts for the group as The Quintet of the Hot Club of France.

Reinhardt's "gypsy jazz" was an instant success, but he also branched out in new directions with delicate Debussy-like compositions such as *Nuages* (*Clouds*) that achieved a following among classical musicians. The poet Jean Cocteau, hearing him in 1931, wrote of "this guitar, which laughs and weeps, a guitar with a human voice."

Django, unfortunately, was all too human. Vain and unreliable, he competed with his colleagues rather than cooperating. In particular, he clashed with the fastidious, sensitive Grappelli. "Stéphane and Django didn't get on very well," said a friend. "The quintet would get a job at some posh place, and the local gypsies would hear about it and when Stéphane went to their dressing room, all these gypsies would be in there. They'd been out stealing chickens and they'd pluck and cook them. Once there was no stove, so they started burning the furniture."

A reckless gambler, Django spent lavishly, buying rounds of calvados for his friends and hiring limousines to drive him to concerts. A dandy, he affected white suits, which he wore with red shoes and black ties. They suited his slicked back hair, his dashing moustache and his taste in women—the wilder and less stylish, the better.

The Quintet was touring England when the Germans invaded France in 1940. Reinhardt spoke no English and felt isolated there. Abandoning the group, he returned home. As Paris was an important rest and recreation

Record Jacket, Django and Grappelli

center for German troops, it was imperative for morale that its clubs, bars and brothels remain open. Many of these, particularly the cellar clubs of Saint-Germain-des-Prés, featured jazz. Hitler decreed that jazz was *entarte*—decadent—and must be stamped out and the racial minorities at the core of the scene be exterminated, but the authorities administering Paris, many of whom enjoyed jazz, chose to ignore this.

Django was permitted to form a new quintet, with clarinettist Hubert Rostaing replacing Grappelli. The Germans required only that he submit his set list for approval before each concert. He found his way round this by disguising American tunes under French titles. *Honeysuckle Rose* was renamed *La Rose de Chèvrefeuille* and *St. Louis Blues* became *La Tristesse de Saint Louis*—The Sadness of Saint Louis.

In 1946, Reinhardt was invited to tour the United States with Duke Ellington, who had heard him during a 1939 visit with his band. Django arrived without a guitar, having been assured he'd be presented with a gold-plated instrument as part of a publicity stunt and be paid for endorsing it. But there was no guitar, so he had to borrow one. To compete with Ellington's orchestra, he had to use an amplified electric guitar, with which he was never comfortable. After the tour, which got tepid reviews, Reinhardt played solo for two weeks in cafés around New York. Fellow guitarist Barney Kessel said, "If Django had wanted to stay in the United States and learn the language, I'm convinced he would have altered the course of contemporary jazz guitar playing—perhaps even the course of the music itself."

Instead Reinhardt returned to France in 1948, announcing he was no longer interested in jazz, switching his focus to art. Retiring to Samois-sur-Seine, near Fontainebleau, he spent most of his time painting female nudes, none of them very accomplished. He died of a cerebral haemorrhage on May 16, 1953, aged only 43. He was survived by a legend and a style of lyrical jazz guitar that has never been surpassed.

THE CELLAR CLUBS OF PARIS

The cellar clubs of Saint-Germain-des-Prés survived through the post-war surge in popularity as U.S. troops replaced the Germans. Many musicians were drawn to the city, including a number of African-Americans, notably Charlie Parker and Bud Powell. Most lived at the Hôtel La Louisiane, (60, rue de Seine, 6th *arrondissement*) and performed at the Club Saint-Germain-des-Prés (13, rue Saint-Benoît, 6th), which was opened in 1947 by the poet Boris Vian. Touring American musicians like Miles Davis played there, as did Rheinhardt. Also popular was the Blue Note Café (27, rue d'Artois, 8th), where pianist Bud Powell recorded an album in 1961. (Footage of Powell at the Blue Note is available on YouTube).

Most clubs closed in the 1950s due to tighter laws on health and safety. A 1961 directory lists, in addition to the Club Saint-Germain-des-Prés and The Blue Note, only four others, the Club du Vieux Colombier, Le Caméléon, Le Chat qui Pêche and Aux Trois Mailletz. Le Chat qui Pêche (4, rue de la Huchette, 1st) still operates as a restaurant, but without music. The others are defunct as jazz venues—for reasons indicated by a 1961 description by American humorist Art Buchwald of the Vieux Colombier: "Hot and always ear-splitting. Another of the student cellars, with the kids raising the roof and the adults sitting in discomfort to watch them do it."

The golden era of jazz in Saint-Germain-des-Prés was celebrated in Bertrand Tavernier's 1986 film *Round Midnight,* based on the friendship between Bud Powell and French jazz fan Francis Paudras. For dramatic purposes, pianist Powell was replaced by tenor saxophonist Dexter Gordon.

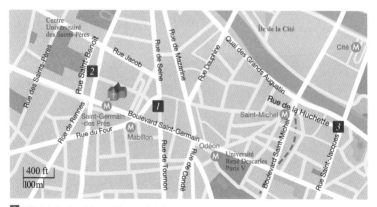

1 Hôtel de La Louisiane: 60, rue de Seine
2 Club Saint-Germain-des-Prés: 13, rue Saint-Benoît
3 Le Chat qui Pêche: 4, rue de la Huchette

J'ai deux Amours

Fox-Trot chanté par **JOSÉPHINE BAKER**

Pour Piano et Chant
6 fr.

Pour Chant seul
1.50

Paroles de
Géo KOGE
et
Henri VAR

Musique de

Vincen
SCOTT

ÉDITION
SALABE
PARIS

Vente en Gros
22, Rue Chauchat - PA
14, Rue de Lorum - BRU

CHAPTER 25.

THE BLACK PEARL

SHE PROVED BLACK WAS BEAUTIFUL

Frida Josephine McDonald was an adequate singer, an average dancer and a mediocre actress. Her taste in men was disastrous, her understanding of finance worse, and she consistently infuriated and frustrated the people with whom she worked. Yet "that bitch Josephine Baker," as the film director Luis Buñuel called her, was also, in the words of Ernest Hemingway, "the most sensational woman anyone ever saw."

Baker was the daughter of an African-American laundress in St. Louis, Missouri. Her father probably belonged to the German family for whom her mother worked. She left school as 12, waited tables, became a chorus girl at 15 and married twice before she was 17, the second time to Pullman porter Willie Baker. She kept his name but abandoned him to perform in the 1921 Broadway revue *Shuffle Along* and the Cotton Club's 1924 show *Chocolate Dandies*. Her dancing skill was limited to simple variations of the Charleston and the Camel Walk, but her gangling movements and goofy grin won her the accolade: "the highest-paid chorus girl in vaudeville."

On October 2, 1925, she was in the company of the *Revue Nègre* when it opened at Paris's Théâtre des Champs-Élysées. Her entrance, naked but for

FÉLICIEN CHAMPSAUR

NORA

la guenon devenue femme

FERENCZI ET FILS, ÉDITEURS
9, rue Antoine-Chantin, 9
PARIS

Cover for the racist novel, *Nora, The Monkey that Became a Woman*, inspired by Baker.

a skirt of feathers, slung over the shoulder of a brawny black man, electrified the audience. Parisians were enchanted by a wised-up black woman whose acrobatic semi-nude dances made a joke of sex yet were intensely provocative. Producers besieged her, as did seducers both male and female, and Josephine, flattered and bisexual, welcomed them all. When the company moved on to Germany, Baker didn't go. Tearing up her contract, she signed with the Folies-Bergère, which built one of its lavish revues around her. The Folies, essentially a music hall, featured a catwalk built high above the audience, and Baker's overhead appearance, near nude, created a sensation in her cheeky costume, a skirt of fat and phallic velvet bananas.

Despite her popularity, Baker was viewed sceptically by many. Racist elements insisted on regarding blacks as intellectually inferior. Novelist Félicien Champsaur published the sensational *Nora, La Guenon Devenue Femme* (*Nora, The She-Monkey Who Became a Woman*). It was inspired by the quack surgery of Serge Voronoff, who claimed to restore failing energy and sexual vigour by transplanting monkey testicles into men. The heroine of *Nora*, born a monkey, evolves into a woman after being implanted with human organs from white donors. The book's cover and illustrations feature a dancer plainly based on Baker, even down to her trademark banana skirt.

Relishing her sexuality, Baker took numerous lovers of both sexes, among them Paul Colin, who designed the posters for her shows, the crime writer Georges Simenon and a Sicilian ex-stonemason, the self-styled "Count" Giuseppe "Pepito" Abatino. Abatino orchestrated her career with skill, attaching her name to a number of ghosted memoirs, confessions and even a novel. With coaching, her thin voice improved sufficiently for her to record six songs for Columbia in Paris in July 1930 including, "*J'ai deux amours*" (I have two loves/My country and Paris), which became a hit, and her lifelong signature tune.

She also starred in the films *La Sirène des Tropiques* (1927), *Zouzou* (1934) and *Princesse Tamtam* (1935). A troublesome performer, she habitually arrived on the set after a sleepless night, accompanied by some of her private menagerie, which included a chimp, a piglet, a goat, a snake, multiple parakeets, fish, three cats, seven dogs and a cheetah named Chiquita, which wore a diamond collar and sometimes escaped, causing panic.

Baker, still a citizen of the United States, returned in 1936, expecting to receive the same acceptance as in France. But the Ziegfeld Follies replaced her after a

Josephine Baker in her famous banana skirt

few weeks with Gypsy Rose Lee, and she encountered racial discrimination and hostile reviews by refusing to play to segregated audiences. On her return to France in 1937, she married a Frenchman and became a French citizen. Remaining in Europe during World War II, she was active as a courier in the Resistance, carrying messages written in invisible ink on her sheet music and also in her underwear. Thanks to "Count" Abatino, she also had entrée to Italian social circles and could pass military information about Mussolini's plans to the Allies. The French government recognised this with various awards, culminating in 1961 with the *Legion d'Honneur*.

Baker had no children but adopted a dozen, each from a different racial group, whom she gathered in the Château des Milandes in Périgord. Maintaining this "World Village" bankrupted her. She was evicted in the 1960s, and her château sold for taxes. Princess Grace of Monaco, the former

Grace Kelly, rescued her, giving her a villa and encouraging her to perform again, starting with a royal gala in Monaco. She also financed Baker's return to the stage in a revue that opened in New York in 1974. The first night audience included Sophia Loren, Mick Jagger, Shirley Bassey, Diana Ross and Liza Minnelli. Baker played New York for a week.

In April 1975, she had just begun a reprise of the same show in Paris, celebrating her half-century on the stage, when she suffered a stroke. *New Yorker* columnist Janet Flanner, a lesbian who acknowledged Baker's sexual appeal, provided her best epitaph: "Her magnificent dark body, a new model to the French, proved for the first time that black was beautiful."

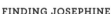

FINDING JOSEPHINE

Josephine Baker was buried in Monaco, at the request of Princess Grace. She has two permanent memorials in Paris. One is a small square, Place Josephine Baker, in Montparnasse, near the theater street of Rue de la Gaite (14th *arrondissement*). The other, oddly, is a public swimming pool, at the Porte de la Gare, in the 13th. Baker had no connection with the area, though the city likes to name public buildings after national heroes and heroines.

In the 1930s, Baker had her own nightclub, Chez Joséphine, at 40, rue Fontaine in the 9th. It advertised "tangos, Charleston, Black bottoms et Jaccob's Jazz." "Jaccob" was Lèon Jacobs, the Belgian bandleader who was her long-time musical director. Most of the theaters and music halls where she performed are still in existence. The Folies-Bergère is located at 8, rue Saulnier in the 9th. The capacious Théâtre des Champs-Elysées, scene of her first triumph, is at 15, avenue Montaigne, in the chic 8th.

The Château des Milandes in Périgord, from which she was evicted, is now a museum of her life, with a collection of personal memorabilia.

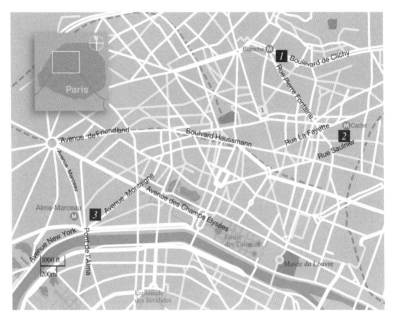

1 Chez Josephine: 40, rue Pierre Fontaine
2 Folies-Bergère: 8, rue Saulnier
3 Théâtre Champs-Élysées: 15, avenue Montaigne

CHAPTER 26.

GENERAL OF THE ARMY OF THE NIGHT

JEAN MOULIN AND THE WORLD WAR II RESISTANCE

On the freezing afternoon of December 19, 1964, André Malraux, minister of culture, mounted the steps of the Pantheon, where the great of France are interred. He delivered a speech still spoken of in awe, celebrating a man who lived in darkness. And though no body was present in the coffin over which he spoke, Malraux bid this shadowy figure enter the hallowed Pantheon: "Enter, with these people born from the shadows and disappeared with them—our brothers in the order of the Night."

Jean Moulin, leader of the World War II resistance against the Nazi occupation, was, in Malraux's phrase, "born of the shadow" and a "brother in the Order of the Night." Despite this, his name is nationally famous. Numerous streets, schools and institutions bear it, and his best-known photograph, showing him in a soft felt hat and trench coat, half-smiling into the camera—the very embodiment of casual courage and Bogart-like cool—is so instantly recognizable it has even appeared on a postage stamp.

When the German army swept across France in 1940, the speed of the Nazi *blitzkrieg* and the total collapse of the armed forces left the nation paralyzed. As the British ferried their troops back home from the beaches at Dunkirk,

Young Resistants from Huelgoat in Brittany

the Germans divided France and installed World War I hero Philippe Pétain at the head of a puppet government in the regional capital of Vichy. Paris was maintained as a rest and recreation resort for his troops, while the remainder of the country became a source of slave labor and a base for Hitler's planned invasions of Britain and North Africa.

The people best fitted to harass the Germans were those who had disapproved of the administration before the war, in particular, the Communists. From among the ranks, Moulin emerged as a natural leader. As assistant to the mayor of the southern city of Montpelier and then sub-mayor of Albertville, he'd helped the international forces fighting the fascist General Francisco Franco during the Spanish Civil War. When the Germans invaded France, he was *prefect* (regional administrator) of the *département* of Eure-et-Loire. Imprisoned and tortured, he tried to cut his throat with a piece of glass rather than sign a document submitting to Vichy control.

Released and deprived of his office, Moulin—now calling himself Joseph Jean Mercier—made his way to London in 1941, where General Charles de Gaulle headed the Free French government in exile. Initially suspicious, since their politics were diametrically opposed, de Gaulle asked Moulin to assess the state of the national resistance to Nazi occupation. Moulin parachuted back into France and began making contact with the bands of partisans known as *maquisards*—people who hid in the *maquis* or undergrowth. He found most of them ineffective, spending as much time fighting among themselves as they did harrying the Germans. Like similar movements in occupied Poland and the Ukraine, France's resistance risked deteriorating into squabbling

Klaus Barbie (center in plain clothes) in Lyon, 1943

rivalries between Communists, Jews, regional nationalists, anarchists and outright gangsters, all of whom pursued rival agendas and often sabotaged each other. One historian observed cynically that, "one could only be a resister if one was maladjusted."

Moulin returned to London in January 1942 with a document called *The Activities, Plans and Requirements of the Groups formed in France*. Impressed and alarmed, de Gaulle asked him to co-ordinate the efforts of the partisan groups. With funds provided by the British government, Moulin was sent back with orders to form an organization that would unite resistance within the occupied zone, gathering intelligence to help the Allies and preparing the ground for the country's eventual re-capture.

Although almost every French person later claimed to have fought the Germans, only about 2 percent of the adult population—about 400,000 people—is believed to have actively participated. After the war, the government formally recognized 220,000 authentic *résistants*. Of these, only a handful pulled a trigger or planted a bomb: Moulin himself killed nobody and never carried a gun. For every armed attack, there were hundreds of minor acts of sabotage: trains derailed, telephone and power lines cut, factory machines disabled. The resistance produced forged papers, ran an "underground railway" to return downed Allied pilots and escaped prisoners of war to England, and operated secret radios to receive coded transmissions from London broadcast over the BBC. Many more helped produce and distribute clandestine newspapers and books; Paris's Editions de Minuit (Midnight Editions) published collections of patriotic poems and even a translation of John Steinbeck's anti-Nazi novel *The Moon Is Down*. Pocket-sized, the books could easily be dropped in the gutter in the event of a search.

Moulin, under the code names "Rex" and "Max," worked tirelessly to coordinate the bickering groups, but the Germans were no less effective. In June 1943, he was arrested in Lyon, probably betrayed by one of his deputies, René Hardy, who had been captured by Klaus Barbie, the head of the Gestapo in Lyon, and agreed to become an informer. Hardy attended the Lyon meeting, but was allowed to escape. Tried twice for collaboration after the war, Hardy was acquitted under dubious circumstances, even though Barbie himself identified him as a traitor.

Brutally tortured, Moulin refused to reveal the secrets of his network. Barbie ordered him taken to Germany for further interrogation, but he is believed to have died on the train. A death certificate filed by the Vichy *Prefect de Police* gives his place of death as Metz, in northeastern France, on the rail route to Germany, but other documents claim he died in Frankfurt, Germany. His body was returned to Paris and cremated. The ashes were placed in a numbered urn in the crematorium at Père Lachaise Cemetery, and remained there until 1964, when de Gaulle, by then President, ordered them transferred to the Pantheon. Whether they were indeed Moulin's ashes, nobody was sure. The doubt merely adds to the shadows around France's ambiguous resistance to Nazi occupation and "the armies of the night" whom Jean Moulin helped to lead.

SEE IT: MEMORIALS TO MOULIN

Reminders of the wartime resistance are hard to avoid in Paris. Scores of plaques on buildings indicate the spots where men and women died during the occupation. On national holidays, each is decorated with flowers. Moulin's ashes are interred in the crypt of the Pantheon. A plaque on the building at 48, rue du Four (6th *arrondissement*) indicates where the first meeting of the Conseil National de la Résistance took place on May 27, 1943.

Musée Jean Moulin

Moulin is commemorated in the Musée Jean Moulin, part of the Museum of the Liberation of France, located at 23, allée de la 2e Division Blindée, in the Jardin Atlantique above the Gare Montparnasse (15th). Along with an account of Moulin's life and death, the museum contains copies of underground newspapers, leaflets, photographs and other materials illustrating the *résistance*.

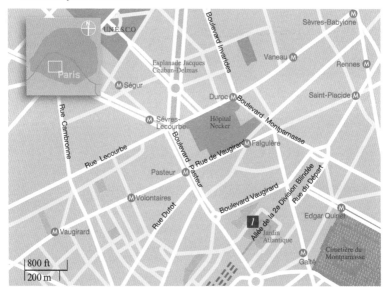

1 Musée Jean Moulin: 23, allée de la 2e Division Blindée

CHAPTER 27

THE GONE WORLD

PARIS AND THE BEAT GENERATION

Since the city of Paris was founded over 2,000 years ago, outsiders have gravitated here, drawn by an atmosphere of what the French called *laissez-faire*—do what you like. After World War II, a few U.S. servicemen, some of them African-American, decided to stay in France. A handful, financed by the G.I. Bill, studied art or the language, but most just hung out, beguiled—as their equivalents had been after World War I—with the wine, the women and the pleasures of a city where almost everything was permitted. By 1948, a group of similarly undirected but creative young outsiders, beatific in their indifference to the material world, was forming in New York's Greenwich Village. Writers Jack Kerouac and John Clellon Holmes coined them a "Beat Generation."

Many of Paris's expatriate bohemians congregated on the left bank, just a few steps from the Seine, where a couple named Rachou ran a tiny establishment in an alley at 9, rue Gît-le-Cœur. Amenities were basic: hole-in-the-floor lavatories, newsprint for toilet paper, leaking roofs, noisy plumbing and sloping floors. Advance notice and an extra payment were required to use the solitary bath. However, it was cheap, and the Rachous were tolerant of the eccentricities of their clients, who included petty

---

‹ Peter Orlovsky and Allen Ginsberg on rue St. André-des-Arts, December 1956. At that time, they were living in Room 25 of the Beat Hotel.

criminals, drug addicts, prostitutes, poets and madmen. Among the other attractions was the ready supply of drugs, particularly hashish. As word spread, the rooms filled with U.S. itinerants, who christened the Rachous's establishment "The Beat Hotel."

The writer William S. Burroughs, who'd been living in Tangier, gravitated there in the late '50s, as did the American poet Allen Ginsberg and his lover Peter Orlovsky. They were joined by painter Brion Gysin, who, with Burroughs, began experimenting with new forms of fiction, cutting up texts and juxtaposing the pieces, with striking effect. Burroughs's "cut up" technique resulted in four novels, *Naked Lunch, Nova Express, The Soft Machine* and *The Ticket That Exploded*, milestones in the development of a new literature.

The novels were scandalous, but Burroughs found a publisher in Maurice Girodias, whose Olympia Press was only five minutes' walk from rue Gît-de-Cœur. At Olympia, Girodias specialised in pornography for the tourist trade, though he also published some books of literary merit, including Nabokov's *Lolita,* Samuel Beckett's *Watt* and *Malloy,* and J.P. Donleavy's *The Ginger Man*. As most Beat authors had no income except for occasional gifts from the United States, Girodias commissioned some to write erotica, which they did under pseudonyms. Terry Southern and Mason Hoffenberg wrote *Candy* as "Matthew Kenton." It became a bestseller. Scots poet Alexander Trocchi wrote *White Thighs* and *Desire and Helen* as "Frances Lengel" and *Thongs* as "Carmencita de Las Lunas." Christopher Logue, later an eminent British poet, compiled two anthologies of erotic limericks and bawdy ballads under the name "Count Palmiro Vicarion."

News of easy money and unlimited dope quickly spread, and the wilder U.S. beats crossed the Atlantic. These included Gregory Corso, fleeing the campaign against drug use sweeping through Greenwich Village and its West Coast equivalent, the San Francisco district of North Beach. Some of the newcomers crowded into the Beat Hotel. Others persuaded George Whitman to let them crash in his nearby Mistral Bookshop.

Racial, sexual or social prejudice was almost unknown in Paris, and the beats found a place where they could thrive. "A writer is esteemed, respected, necessary to the intellectual life of his country," said novelist

William Styron. Homosexuality had been decriminalised by the Napoleonic code, so Ginsberg and Orlovsky could share a bed, sometimes even squeezing in a third participant.

William Burroughs at the Beat Hotel, 1958.

"There is such an absence of race hate that it seems a little unreal," said novelist Richard Wright. And though blacks made up a large part of the American community in France, Chester Himes had trouble finding a hotel to accept himself and his white girlfriend, until he tried the Rachous. After that he moved into the Hôtel La Louisiane, a popular hangout for black jazz musicians like Bud Powell, Miles Davis and Charlie Parker; it was close to the cellar clubs of Saint-Germain-des-Prés, where they played most nights. To socialize, Wright, Himes and James Baldwin met halfway to Montparnasse, in the Café de Tournon on the edge of the Luxembourg Gardens.

The Beats admired previous generations of literary rebels, like the Surrealists and Dadaists, but even though many major figures were still living and working in Paris, the few attempts at meeting were disastrous. The newcomers did not speak French and ill-understood the importance even one-time bohemians could place on formality. When a French friend invited Corso, Ginsberg and Burroughs to a party to meet Marcel Duchamp, Man Ray and Benjamin Peret, the young men arrived drunk. Ginsberg knelt in front of Duchamp and tried to kiss his knees, as Scott Fitzgerald had done when he met James Joyce. Duchamp just thought he was crazy, an impression reinforced when Corso cut off part of his tie as a souvenir.

At a preview of John Huston's film *The Roots of Heaven*, Burroughs tried, without success, to convince the director to make a film about life in Tangier as seen by an addict desperately seeking drugs. Another member of the group, B.J. Carroll, emptied a glass of champagne over the head of the film's star Errol Flynn. Security guards tossed him into the Seine.

Each room at the Richous contained a gas ring, and Burroughs, who had a sweet tooth, sometimes cooked up *majoun,* or drug candy, from hashish or cannabis, mixed with cinnamon, nutmeg, caraway seeds and honey. When Gertrude Stein's elderly companion Alice B. Toklas appealed for recipes for a cookbook, Brion Gysin playfully sent this one, calling it "Hashish Fudge—which," he suggested, "anyone could whip up on a rainy day … it might provide an entertaining refreshment for a Ladies' Bridge Club … In Morocco it is thought to be good for warding off the common cold in damp winter weather." Toklas included it in *The Alice B. Toklas Cookbook.* Nervous editors removed the recipe from later editions, but for a while the lives of America's club ladies must have become considerably more interesting.

As the '60s marched on, so did the Beats. Burroughs found himself in London, while Ginsberg traveled to India and eventually the U.K. The Beat Hotel closed in the spring of 1963, but its literary ghosts still haunt Paris.

SEE IT: BEAT PARIS

The run-down Beat Hotel has become the luxurious Relais Hôtel du Vieux Paris, though a plaque celebrates one-time tenants Burroughs, Gysin, Ginsberg, Orlovsky, Harold Norse and Ian Sommerville.

A plaque honoring the tenants of the Beat Hotel

George Whitman acquired the name of Sylvia Beach's Shakespeare and Company in the mid-1950s and his Mistral Bookshop still operates under that name (37, rue de la Bûcherie, 5th *arrondissement*). The store is still managed by his daughter, Sylvia Beach Whitman, and the shop and nearby park is the venue for a biannual literary festival. The shop, which contains some souvenirs of visitors like Burroughs, still maintains a tradition of offering a bed to visiting writers in return for light work.

If you can get your hands on a copy, Olympia Press first editions of Burroughs, Corso and Southern now command high prices. Of particular interest are the four Burroughs titles, Gregory Corso's *American Express,* with a photo of the author on the dust wrapper, and the Southern/Hoffenberg *Candy,* particularly the later printing, for which Girodias, hoping to fool the police, who had banned it, changed the title to *Lollipop.*

Although the English bookshop on rue de Seine no longer exists, the Hôtel de La Louisiane (60, rue de Seine, 6th) remains in business, as does the popular Café de Tournon, which still flourishes as Comptoir Tournon (18, rue Tournon, 6th).

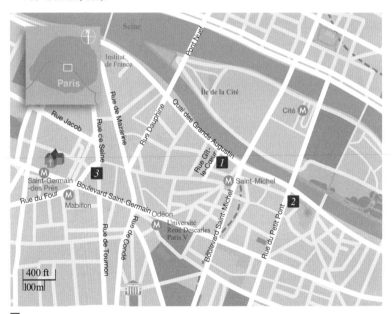

1 Beat Hotel: 9, rue Gît-le-Coeur
2 Shakespeare and Company: 37, rue de la Bûcherie
3 Hôtel de La Louisiane: 60, rue de Seine

aandeløs

a bout de souffle

med
JEAN SEBERG

JEAN-PAUL BELMONDO

iscenesat af
JEAN-LUC GODARD

drejebog
FRANÇOIS TRUFFAUT

kunstnerisk og teknisk raadgiver
CLAUDE CHABROL

med
Henri-Jacques HUET
Liliane DAVID
Claude MANSARD
VAN DOUDE
Daniel BOULANGER

Tildelt SØLVBJØRNEN ved
BERLINALEN 1960
PRODUKTION
GEORGES DE BEAUREGARD
ENERET
TEATRENES FILMS - KONTOR ⅍

musik
MARTIAL SOLAL
kamera
Raoul COUTARD

CHAPTER 28

NEW WAVE

TRUTH 24 TIMES A SECOND

Rue Campagne-Première, a quiet side street in Montparnasse, seems an unlikely location for a moment in cinema history—which was why Jean-Luc Godard chose it for the climactic scene of his 1960 film *À Bout de Souffle* (*Breathless*). Jean-Paul Belmondo, playing a small-time crook on the run, is shot down by the police and dies at the corner of boulevard Raspail. His last words are a snarl at the American girl whom he thinks has betrayed him: *"C'est vraiment dégueulasse."* Though the saying has been translated different ways—the Criterion Collection print of the film uses "You make me want to puke"—it has became an emblem of the movement Godard helped create: the *nouvelle vague* or New Wave.

In the space of two or three years, a handful of young French directors re-wrote the grammar of film. Traditionally, movie production required a hundred technicians, a sound stage, tons of equipment and, of course, stars. But *À Bout de Souffle* had none of these except for Jean Seberg as the girl. Godard realized that, because of lightweight cameras, sensitive tape recorders and fast films developed for combat and TV shooting, a movie could be shot by five or six people working by daylight on an ordinary street. Editing, he saved screen time and forced the pace by ignoring

‹ *À Bout de Souffle* (*Beathless*), directed by Jean-Luc Godard and starring (from left) Jean-Paul Belmondo and Jean Seberg, 1960.

traditional fades and dissolves, and "jump cutting" between scenes. Movies were never the same again.

Revolutions, like brush fires, start with a spark, but explode only if the forest is ready to burn. The *nouvelle vague* began with the contrarian views of some young Paris critics—but since the cultural forest was tinder-dry, the blaze they lit raced round the world. The critics included Jean-Luc Godard, Jacques Rivette, Éric Rohmer, Claude Chabrol, Alain Resnais and François Truffaut. Truffaut emerged as their star. His instinctive sense of cinema was rooted in an unhappy childhood, marred by episodes of truancy and petty theft, from which he had taken refuge in the darkness of the movie house. When he directed his first feature, based on this delinquent childhood, he called it *The Four Hundred Blows*, street slang for "raising hell".

At 18, without education or prospects, Truffant joined the army, hated it, deserted and ended up in military prison. He was rescued by the film critic André Bazin, who gave him a job writing reviews for his magazine. Truffaut joined the group of young *cinéastes*—movie buffs—who hung out at the Cinémathèque Française, the cinema under the film museum in the Palais de Chaillot. The cinema's director, lumbering, unkempt and opinionated Henri Langlois, became their mentor. Each day, he presented a non-stop series of screenings—1940s American B-Westerns alternated with silent French classics and Soviet propaganda. Langlois offered no theories, leaving his young followers to make up their own minds.

Truffaut and his friends wrangled over what made a film good or bad in face-to-face debates and in articles for magazines like *Cahiers du Cinéma*. Into the "bad" category went France's sober post-war productions they called *le cinema de papa*: daddy's movies. Truffaut's 1954 essay "A Certain Tendency in French Cinema," attacked the respectful adaptations of "great" novels that were the backbone of the business. Though neither Chabrol nor Truffaut spoke much English, all agreed that the "good" films were the fast, cheap, confident products of Hollywood: Westerns, wisecracking comedies and the urban crime movies they christened "black" or "dark," *film noir*.

The directors of the New Wave had little in common socially or politically, except for their boredom with the French film industry and a conviction that it could be improved. Even the label *"nouvelle vague"* was applied by

Director François Truffaut on the set of *Fahrenheit 451*, 1966

accident. Journalist Françoise Giroud of *L'Express* coined it to describe all creative young French people, but the filmmakers made it their own. None set out to become a filmmaker. Chabrol was studying pharmacy. Godard, the son of a wealthy Swiss doctor, wrote publicity for a distributor of American films. More political than the others, he embraced revolution, strewing slogans in his wake. He called his generation "the children of Marx and Coca-Cola" and wrote "If a photograph is truth, then the cinema is truth 24 times a second." When someone demanded, "You must agree that a story should have a beginning, middle, and end," Godard retorted: "Certainly — though not necessarily in that order."

Each of these young artists found his own way to make his first film. Chabrol used an inheritance to bankroll *Le Beau Serge*, and Godard worked as a building laborer to finance *À Bout de Souffle*. Truffaut, a lifelong womanizer, married Madeleine Morgenstern, whose father was one of France's biggest film distributors. Tired of Truffaut's tirades, Morgenstern *père* challenged him to do better. Having been banned from the 1959 Cannes Festival for his insulting reviews, Truffaut returned in 1960 and won the Best Director prize for *The Four Hundred Blows* and the prestigious Palme d'Or for best film.

The Four Hundred Blows

Just as he had been the most outspoken of the group in his writings, Truffaut became the most inventive as a filmmaker—and the most commercially successful. Foreign audiences enjoyed his witty re-working of Hitchcock-style menace in *The Bride Wore Black,* his respectful adaptation of a French literary classic in *Jules and Jim* and his celebration of filmmaking in *Day for Night*, in which he starred as the harassed director of the film within the film. He also played the UFO investigator Lacombe in Steven Spielberg's *Close Encounters of the Third Kind*. His enemies, who soon included his old colleague Godard, sneered that he'd become what he once attacked. They called him the '60s equivalent of the frothiest and most sentimental of all pre-war directors, René Clair. Truffaut ignored them and just kept filming.

Throughout his life, Truffaut had a voracious sexual appetite and was an unrepentant patron of prostitutes and brothels. He inspired the character of the relentless seducer of his own 1977 film *The Man Who Loved Women*—a man whose last thought before dying is of the legs of a nurse. His greatest success, both on and off the screen, invariably involved actresses. He electrified the careers of Catherine Deneuve, her sister Françoise Dorléac, Isabelle Adjani, Fanny Ardant, Jeanne Moreau and Jacqueline Bisset by casting them against type, and, usually, by seducing them as well.

In 1967, he fell in love with 19-year-old Claude Jade on the set of *Stolen Kisses,* proposed marriage and spent considerable effort convincing her stern provincial family he had reformed. Her wedding dress was already made when the firing of Henri Langlois from the Cinémathèque helped spark the revolution of 1968. After he and other members of the *Cahiers* group prevented the opening of that year's Cannes Festival by clinging to the curtains of the festival cinema, Truffaut told Jade he'd changed his mind; the revolution made marriage unimportant. Everyone shrugged and said, "That's François," even Jade, who worked with him on two more films.

So great was Truffaut's energy that everyone believed he would defeat a brain tumor, diagnosed when he turned 50. He died two years later, in 1984, leaving his mistress, the actress Fanny Ardant, pregnant with a daughter.

Even in death, he didn't invite solemnity. For an epitaph, one could do worse than quote an exchange from *Day for Night*. The anguished male star, dumped by his girlfriend, buttonholes colleagues to ask them "Are women magic?" "No," one replies instantly. "Just their legs."

CINÉMATHÈQUE FRANÇAISE

The Cinémathèque Française is one of the world's leading archives dedicated to the preservation and presentation of film.

Since 2005, it has been located in Paris's 12th arrondissement, in a postmodern building designed by architect Frank Gehry.

Cinémathèque Française
51, rue de Bercy
12th *arrondissement*
www.cinematheque.fr

SEE IT: PARIS ON FILM

The love affair between Paris and movies goes back to the very beginnings of cinema. The first public film screening, by the Lumière brothers, took place in the Salon Indien of the Grand Café on Place de l'Opéra on December 28, 1895. Location shooting around the city soon became commonplace and certain sites familiar. René Clair shot *Paris qui Dort* on the Eiffel Tower in 1925 and Charles Laughton starred as writer

Paris qui Dort, 1925

Georges Simenon's Inspector Maigret in 1949 in *The Man on the Eiffel Tower*. Fred Astaire and Audrey Hepburn danced on the landmark in *Funny Face* (1957), Grace Jones descended from it by paraglider in the James Bond film *A View to a Kill* (1985) and it was eaten by a virus from outer space in *The Day the Earth Stood Still* (2008).

The nearby Bir-Hakeim bridge, with its elevated railway, has also been extremely popular in film. Marlon Brando crossed it to meet Maria Schneider in *Last Tango in Paris* (1972), it became a fruit and vegetable market where Eric Bana and Mathieu Amalric bargain for terrorist information in Steven Spielberg's *Munich* (2005) and Ellen Page shows off her dream-building skill there to Leonardo DiCaprio in *Inception* (2010).

^ *Charade*, 1963

Likewise, many scenes have been set on the *bateaux mouche* tour boats that pass under the bridge, including *Charade* (1963) with Cary Grant and Audrey Hepburn and *Paris Blues* with Sidney Poitier. Liam Neeson leaps from a bridge onto a cabin cruiser to rescue his daughter in *Taken* (2008). Other scenes take place on *chalands* or freight barges, including Audrey Hepburn fishing in *Funny Face* (1957), Harrison Ford held prisoner in *Frantic* (1988) and Jean Vigo's touching *L'Atalante* (1934), about a barge captain and his new wife.

The city's streets have proven good locations for car chases. Neeson spreads destruction across most of Paris in *Taken*, as does Matt Damon in *The Bourne Identity*, ...*Supremacy*

Café des Deux Moulins

and ...*Ultimatum* (2002, 2004 and 2007). *Ronin* (1998) with Robert DeNiro makes imaginative but violent use of the Voies sur Berge, the carriageway running by the edge of the Seine. More imaginative uses of locations include the Centre Pompidou, which became a rocket-making factory in the Bond movie *Moonraker* (1979).

The Arc de Triomph is another popular location. Alain Delon flies a light aircraft through the arch in *Les Aventuriers* (1967) and Edward Fox comes close to killing President de Gaulle there in *The Day of the Jackal* (1973).

The café, that eternal symbol of Paris, is a popular location as well. In *Le Fabuleux Destin de Amélie Poulain* (2001), Amélie works in the Café des Deux Moulins, 15, rue Lepic in Montmartre (18th), though most of the film's interiors were actually shot in Germany. In *À Bout de Souffle* (1960), Jean-Paul Belmondo buys the *Herald Tribune* from Jean Seberg on the Champs-Élysées and dies in front of Man Ray's studio at 31, rue Campagne-Première (14th).

Tomb of Oscar Wilde

Many directors have used Paris cemeteries, in particular Père-Lachaise (5, boulevard de Ménilmontant, 20th). The tomb of Oscar Wilde features in *Jules et Jim* (1962) and an episode of the omnibus film *Paris, Je t'aime* (2006), with episodes shot in almost every *arrondissement*, including one set in the Montparnasse Cemetery at the graves of Jean-Paul Sartre and Simone de Beauvoir.

CHAPTER 29.

BEAUTY IS IN THE STREETS
THE STUDENT REVOLUTION OF 1968

Since 1782, when Marie Antoinette ordered a theater built on the edge of the Luxembourg Gardens, the Théâtre de l'Odéon has witnessed few scenes stranger than those of May 1968. That spring, its columned portico seethed with students from the nearby Sorbonne, engaged in heated political argument. Some wore costumes looted from the theater's wardrobe department. Roman robes from the plays of Racine mixed with 18th-century court dress suitable for Beaumarchais—a visual metaphor for the theatrical nature of this improbable uprising.

The unusual events of 1968 began on March 22, in the bleak concrete suburb of Nanterre. Student leader Daniel Cohn-Bendit interrupted the speech of a minister opening a new university swimming pool to protest that male students were not allowed in the female dormitories. The incident sent shock waves through an academic community that shunned controversy.

Overnight, Cohn-Bendit, dubbed "Dani the Red" because of his politics and red hair, became a star. He was joined by Jacques Sauvageot, Alain Geismar and Alain Krivine in what became known as the "Movement of the 22 March."

Among the children of the post-war baby boom, his gesture fanned a smoldering resentment of the repressive regime of President Charles de Gaulle. A refusal to lower the voting age from 21, a stifling control of the media—in particular the country's sole TV station, ORTF—and a resistance to new political and social ideas contributed to the general frustration. It was exacerbated by a stodgy curriculum in the universities and an aging faculty. The university authorities also raised tempers by trivial restrictions like a ban on the *monome*, a rowdy conga-like parade through the city with which students had traditionally celebrated their graduation.

Poster produced by students during the 1968 riots, showing a woman throwing a paving stone at police. The slogan translates as "Beauty is in the Streets."

Because Cohn-Bendit's parents had fled Hitler to live in France, the head of the French Communist Party, Georges Marchais, dismissed him as a "German anarchist." Students at the Sorbonne, sensing the implied anti-Semitic slur and chanting "We Are All German Jews," went on strike on May 2. Needing a venue in which to meet, they demanded access to the nearby Théâtre de l'Odéon, which veteran actor/manager Jean-Louis Barrault leased from the state. Anxious to be seen as up-to-date, he turned over the building to them, and even made a speech denouncing "bourgeois culture." He was horrified as the invaders destroyed sets, ripped up the red velvet seats, and looted the wardrobe department, stealing the best costumes and fouling the rest.

With conspicuously poor timing, Minister of Culture André Malraux chose this moment to dismiss Henri Langlois as head of the Cinémathèque Française, claiming—with some justice—that he flouted civil service rules.

Furious at this treatment of their mentor, the directors of the *nouvelle vague,* including François Truffaut, Jean-Luc Godard and Louis Malle, converged on Cannes and halted the film festival by physically clinging to the curtains in the main cinema. At the Cinémathèque itself, Truffaut's favorite actor, Jean-Pierre Leaud, made a

Small stone blocks that paved the city's streets.

fiery speech that ended when the Compagnies Républicaines de Sécurité, France's national guard, charged the crowd.

In steel helmets and gas masks, carrying riot shields and wielding club-like *matraques,* the CRS personified repression. In calling them out, the government escalated the conflict. Students felled the big chestnut trees lining boulevard Saint-Michel, creating barricades from behind which they jeered that "CRS" stood for *"Connards, Racistes et Salopards"* (Assholes, Racists and Bastards). They also tore up the small stone blocks that paved the city's streets and flung them, with devastating effect.

Radical elements in the labor movement, particularly in the automobile companies, saw this disorder as an opportunity and demanded higher wages, better conditions and greater employee control. When even their own unions disagreed, they went on strike and occupied the factories. The left-wing political parties were powerless against this popular expression of frustration, particularly when student leaders and intellectuals formed an unlikely alliance with the factory workers, coaching them in Marxist/ Leninist rhetoric. The railways, newspapers and post offices shut down. ORTF went off the air. The banks also closed. France was paralyzed.

Without TV or the press to rally their followers, the protestors fell back on the public meeting and the march. Meanwhile, Paris's largest art school, the École des Beaux-Arts, began printing posters that soon covered the walls of the city. Quickly and simply produced, they were often masterpieces of propaganda. A face bloodied by a *matraque* glared out under the slogan

École des Beaux-Arts

"Bourgeois, You Have Understood Nothing." Another poster caught a girl in the act of flinging a stone, with the slogan "*La beauté est dans la rue*" — "Beauty Is In The Streets."

On May 29, de Gaulle and his family boarded two military helicopters and took off for an unknown destination, carrying all his official papers and leaving the Élysée Palace deserted. Even his Prime Minister, George Pompidou, had no idea where he had gone. From his undisclosed hideout, de Gaulle refused to return as long as disorder continued. Ordinary people were stunned by the prospect of life without the man who had become a symbol of France. Hundreds of thousands paraded— not against the general, but in support.

De Gaulle's refuge was Baden-Baden in Germany, where he met with Jacques Massu, commander of French forces. General Massu assured him the army was loyal and would, if necessary, put down the protestors. Returning to France after three days, de Gaulle dissolved parliament and announced elections for June. The dissidents expected a left-wing landslide. Instead, Gaullists were re-elected with a huge majority. Voters preferred someone who would restore TV and the daily paper, collect the garbage, re-open the banks and make the trains run again.

Time brought most of the demanded reforms. De Gaulle retired in 1969, to be replaced by the more liberal Pompidou. The voting age was lowered to 18 and universities were modernized. Henri Langlois was reinstated to the Cinémathèque and the Cannes festival undertook to show more films by new directors. Though Malraux refused to renew Jean-Louis Barrault's lease on the Odéon Théâtre, the actor resourcefully moved to the basement of the derelict Gare d'Orsay railway station. It was soon one of the city's most progressive venues.

Radicals settled down to being solid citizens. Daniel Cohn-Bendit went on to an active political career as member of the European Parliament and a major spokesperson for the Green movement. Most *soixante-huitards* look back on the revolt with nostalgia, as the last moment when France showed some of the spirit that motivated the Commune and the uprising of 1789. But it was hardly a *real* revolution, they insist, and speak of it only as *les evénéments* (the events) of 1968.

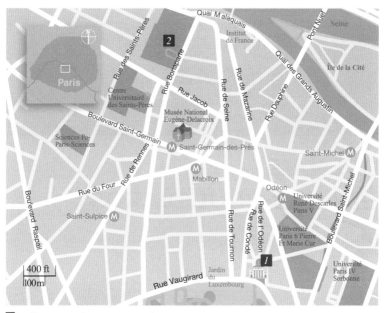

1 Théâtre de l'Odéon: Place de l'Odéon
2 École des Beaux-Arts: 14, rue Bonaparte

OPÉRA & GRANDS BOULEVARDS

1 La Comédie-Française: Place Colette
2 Palais Royal
3 *Les Deux Plateaux*: Cour d'Honneur
4 Colette Apartment: 9, rue Beaujolais
5 Restaurant Grand Vérfour: 17, rue Beaujolais
6 Passages Vivienne and Colbert
7 Office of Eugène-Fraçois Vidocq: 13, passage Vivienne
8 Bibliothèque Nationale
9 Le Chabanais: 12, rue Chabanais
10 Lully Apartment: 45, rue des Petits-Champs
11 Harry's New York Bar: 5, rue Daunou
12 Café de la Paix: Corner of Place de l'Opéra and boulevard des Capucines
13 Palais Garnier: Corner of rue Scribe and rue Auber
14 Galeries Lafayette: 40, boulevard Haussmann

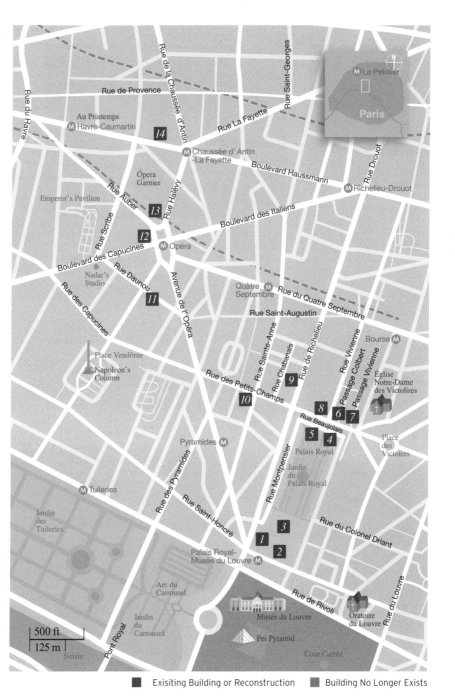

Exisiting Building or Reconstruction   Building No Longer Exists

START:
Métro at Palais Royal

MÉTRO:
① or ⑦

END:
Métro at Chaussée
d'Antin–La Fayette

MÉTRO:
⑦ or ⑨

Palais Royal in the 18th century

Once Napoleon III commissioned a new home for the Paris Opéra (opened in 1875), the area surrounding Charles Garnier's sumptuous creation became the most fashionable in the city. Department stores and banks appeared along the new boulevards and cafés blossomed in the local squares. Tenements gave way to expensive apartment buildings. The right bank of the Seine provided a luxurious setting for the explosion of music, fashion and culture known as *la Belle Époque*– the beautiful era–which made Paris, until the beginning of World War I, the most glamorous city in the world.

Leave Métro at Palais Royal (Lines ① and ⑦) and enter Place de Palais-Royal.

Victor Hugo

1 La Comédie-Française, the French national theater, is located at 2, rue Richelieu on Place Colette. The company was formed in 1680, when Louis XIV combined the troupe of the playwright Molière and its rivals. Initially, it performed opposite the Café Procope on rue de l'Ancienne-Comédie (the street of the old Comédie). Since 1799, it has occupied the former theater of the Palais Royal, designed by Victor Louis. Members of the company enjoy a privileged existence, particularly if invited to become *sociétaires*, with a share of the profits and, after 20 years, a pension. In 1974, 18-year-old Isabelle Adjani created a scandal when she refused such a contract, preferring a film career. Productions are entirely in French, and stress the classical repertoire: Corneille, Racine, Molière, Marivaux, Feydeau and other French classics. The theater offers visits with a talk that traces its history through its collection of paintings, documents and designs. **www.comedie-francaise.fr**

Cross Place de Palais-Royal and enter gardens of Palais Royal.

Cardinal Richelieu

2 Originally the home of Cardinal Richelieu and known as the Palais-Cardinal, the Palais Royal, completed in 1639, today houses the Conseil d'État, the Constitutional Council and the Ministry of Culture. Though the gardens are open to the public, the palace itself does not allow visitors.

Until the Revolution, various royals occupied the palace, most notably Philippe, Duc d'Orléans, who, as a gesture to the politics of the time, took the name "Philippe Égalité" (Equality Philip). He opened the gardens to the public and built the colonnades that enclose them on three sides, creating a popular social and shopping center, as well as a haunt of gamblers, pimps and prostitutes; Marie Duplessis, la Dame aux Caméllias, met her first protector here. During the 20th century, the elegance of the gardens was restored with the creation of fountains and the planting of a central *allée* of lime trees.

Palais Royal, circa 1865

3 The area in front of the Ministry of Culture, the Cour d'honneur, is dominated by Daniel Buren's 1986 sculpture *Les Deux Plateaux* (The Two Levels); so named because it comprises 200 striped columns above-ground and water running under grilles below. The fountain of silver spheres is by Pol Bury.

The Cour d'honneur is lined with the Colonnades of the Palais Royal; antique shops, fashion boutiques and restaurants occupy what used to be gambling houses and seedy cafés.

Colette

Exit Palais Royal onto rue de Beaujolais. This area was home to such writers as Jean Cocteau and Sidionie-Gabrielle Colette and was also used as a setting by many others, including Honoré de Balzac (*Le Pere Goriot*) and Henry James *(The American)*.

4 The author known simply as Colette lived at 9, rue de Beaujolais from 1927 to 1930 and from 1938 until her death in 1954. It was here that she wrote *Gigi,* adapted into a popular musical and film. During 1940, she was often visited by Jean Cocteau, who rented an apartment nearby at 36, rue Montpensier.

5 Opened in 1784, Restaurant Grand Véfour (17, rue de Beaujolais) is one of Paris's most venerable and expensive eating-places. Napoleon dined here with Joséphine and, according to legend, proposed marriage. Brass nameplates on the tables identify other clients, including Victor Hugo, Honoré de Balzac, George Sand, André Malraux, Jean-Paul Sartre and Simone de Beauvoir. Jean Cocteau drawings decorate the menus.

Exit rue Beaujolais, cross rue des Petits-Champs and enter Passage Vivienne.

6 The adjoining Passage Vivienne and Passage Colbert are glass-roofed 19th century shopping arcades housing fashion boutiques (Jean Paul Gaultier) and restaurants (Le Grand Colbert, used as a movie location in films such as *Something's Gotta Give*). The original tile floors of the Galleries are by mosaicist Giandomenico Facchina, whose signature appears in several places. Symbols of industry and commerce—cornucopias, anchors and beehives—decorate the walls.

7 At the top of the spiral staircase, 13, passage Vivienne was the offices of the first private detective, Eugène-Fraçois Vidocq, from 1833 to 1847. Vidocq was the inspiration for Edgar Allan Poe's C. Auguste Dupin in *The Murders in the Rue Morgue* and *The Purloined Letter.*

Exit passage Vivienne onto rue Vivienne and turn left.

13, Passage Vivienne, 1906

On rue Vivienne

Edward VII's bathtub at Le Chabanis

8 Opposite is the site of the original Bibliothèque Nationale or National Library, now relocated at Tolbiac. The bronze statue of the walking man visible in the rear courtyard is of Jean-Paul Sartre.

Enter rue des Petits-Champs and turn right. Continue along rue des Petits-Champs and take second right into rue Chabanais.

9 Le Chabanais, Paris's most famous brothel was formerly located at 12, rue Chabanais. From 1878 to 1946, it provided unparalleled services for generations of aristocrats, intellectuals and crowned heads. The anonymous owners, who included members of the exclusive club Le Jockey, furnished it with antiques, including an entire room in the Japanese style that had won first prize at the 1896 Universal Exposition. Others rooms were decorated as Arab tents, 18th-century boudoirs and the cabin of an ocean liner, while its wardrobe included appropriate costumes for all. For the Prince of Wales, later Edward VII, it provided an ornate metal bath in which his favorite girl bathed in champagne while the prince and his friends sat around and drank from it. On his first visit to Paris, Salvador Dalí asked to be taken there. After two hours, he left "with enough to last me for the rest of my life in the way of accessories to furnish, in less than a minute, no matter what erotic reverie, even the most exacting." Le Chabanais, like all such establishments in France, was closed in 1946, and turned into student housing.

Return to rue des Petits-Champs.

10 Jean-Baptiste Lully, court composer to Louis XIV, lived at 45, rue des Petits-Champs. He died bizarrely after crushing a toe by too violent use of

the heavy staff with which he beat time
while conducting.

Enter avenue de l'Opéra and turn right. Cross to
rue Daunou, on your left.

11 Opened in 1911, Harry's New York Bar
(5, rue Daunou) featured a swinging door and other
mahogany furnishings imported from a Manhattan
bar to create an authentic atmosphere. The bar was
an institution in the 1920s and 1930s and clients
included boxers Primo Carnera and Jack Dempsey,
actors Humphrey Bogart and Rita Hayworth,
and George Gershwin, who composed part of his
symphonic poem *An American in Paris* at the
bar's basement piano. Harry's is credited with the
invention of the Bloody Mary, the French 75 and
the Sidecar.

Return to avenue de l'Opéra, and continue to
Place de l'Opéra.

Then & Now

Passage Vivienne c. 1890

Bibliotheque Nationale c. 1890

Café de la Paix, 1911

Émile Zola

Nana by Édouard Manet

12 The corner of place de l'Opéra and boulevard des Capucines is home to the Grand Hotel and Café de la Paix. Designed by Charles Garnier, architect of the Paris Opéra opposite, the Grand (then the Grand Hôtel-de-la-Paix) was Paris's first large modern hotel. Opened on June 30, 1862, it was popular with army officers who hired rooms to entertain their women and indulge in absinthe and cocaine. Émile Zola, a client of the café, set the climax of his 1880 novel *Nana* in one such room, where Nana's fellow *cocottes* gather to watch her die from smallpox.

In the novel, Zola links Nana's rise and fall to the 1867 Exposition Universelle, which, because of an influx of foreign visitors, made the Grand the most fashionable hotel in Paris. Its café thrived as well. In 1874, sculptor Frédéric Bartholdi met members of the Franco-American Union here to plan his *Liberty Enlightening the World*, better known as the Statue of Liberty. Composer Jules Massenet and ballet impresario Serge Diaghilev were also clients, as was Edward VII.

In April 1896, only four months after Auguste and Louis Lumière presented the first public film screening at the nearby Salon Indien (14, boulevard des Capucines, now Hôtel Scribe), their rival Eugène Pirou hired the Café de la Paix to screen *Le Coucher de la Marie* (The Bride Goes to Bed), a striptease film which, though modest by today's standards, was banned in many places.

In the 1920s, the café was patronized by Josephine Baker and Ernest Hemingway, who wrote in the story *My Old Man* of sitting with his father on the terrace—a location where, traditionally, if you waited long enough, you met everyone you had ever known. In his 1921, *The Absinthe Drinkers,*

Canadian poet Robert W. Service described a "little wizened Spanish man" who waits there, year after year, to kill an enemy, explaining, "for has it not been ever said that all the world one day/Will pass in pilgrimage before the Café de la Paix?"

13 The Palais Garnier—also known as the Opéra de Paris or Opéra Garnier—didn't open until 1875, though construction was begun in 1862. During the Prussian Siege of 1871, the unfinished building became a warehouse. The subsequent Commune further delayed construction. Captured Communards were imprisoned in the cellars that, after 1909, became notorious as the domain of the Phantom in Gaston Leroux's *The Phantom of the Opera*. Once completed, however, the lavishness of its interior and of its productions created a legend.

The Opéra Garnier c. 1896

On the building's façade, marble friezes, columns and statuary portray metaphorical or mythological figures. The central group on the roof depicts the god Apollo, flanked by the muses of Poetry and Music. Giant gilded figures by Charles Gumery at each end of the pediment represent Harmony and Poetry. Lower groups symbolize Instrumental Music and Lyrical Drama. The sculpture on the right side of the entrance, Jean-Baptiste Carpeaux's 1869 *The Dance*, depicting a nude god rattling a tambourine while naked girls dance around him, was called indecent and pelted with ink. Garnier asked Gumery to create a more modest group, but the Franco-Prussian War intervened and it was never replaced.

The Opéra's grand staircase is 30 meters (98 feet) high, with polychrome marble balustrades. The branching staircase is famously descended by the Phantom at the Opéra ball; Audrey Hepburn also flounces down these steps to the music of Wagner

The inauguration of the Opéra 1890–1900

Funny Face, 1957

Opera model

in *Funny Face*. On ceremonial occasions, guards in silver breastplates line the staircase, while the official party greets guests on the *palier* or landing.

Garnier intended the chandelier-lit main foyer, 54 meters long, to rival the Palace of Versailles in opulence. Mosaics by Georges Clairin decorate the ceiling. Its 33 paintings took Paul Baudry nine years to complete. Michael Powell and Emeric Pressburger use the space for the rehearsal scene in *The Red Shoes* when Ludmilla Tchérina announces her engagement.

The auditorium is a classic "golden horseshoe," 30 meters wide, 32 meters deep and 20 meters high, decorated with gilded putti and lit by a six-ton chandelier. At 60 meters high, the stage can accommodate 450 performers. Of the 1,600 seats, all upholstered in red velvet, the best are in the boxes—patrons wished to be seen as much as to see, after all. The ceiling was repainted in 1964 by Marc Chagall in a style regarded by many as inconsistent with the rest of the building.

Housed in the Emperor's Rotunda high above rue Scribe, the Opéra's library contains 80,000 scores and books, and 25,000 sketches, costumes and scale models. Many of the best items are displayed in special exhibitions at the museum.

In 1990, the Paris opera company moved to a new home at Bastille. The Palais Garnier now mainly presents ballet. It encourages visitors, and guided tours are also offered. **www.operadeparis.fr**

Exit Opéra onto rue Scribe, and then walk to boulevard Haussmann.

14 Located at 40, boulevard Haussmann, the Galeries Lafayette is one of the world's premier department stores. In 1893, Théophile Bader and his cousin Alphonse Kahn opened a fashion store at the corner of rue La Fayette and rue de la Chaussée d'Antin. In 1896, they purchased the entire building and in 1905 a number of others nearby. Georges Chedanne was commissioned to design a new store. He exploited the structural possibilities of cast iron, pioneered by Gustave Eiffel, to create a 10-story cylindrical space, topped by a dome of colored glass and steel. (To demonstrate its faith in its safety, in 1919 the store offered 25,000 francs to any pilot who landed on the roof.) Chedanne added cast-iron balconies, and a staircase on branching iron columns, both in the style known as Art Nouveau, the "new art" that replaced traditional Italianate forms with flowing shapes inspired by vines and flowers.

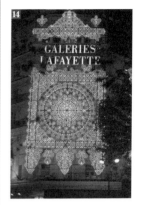

Later, Chedanne's pupil Ferdinand Chanut, an enthusiast for oriental bazaars, divided the store into an eventual 96 departments, including haberdashery, photography, lighting, furniture, travel items and toys, to which were added a library, a hair salon and a café which continues to offer a spectacular view from the roofs to the Eiffel Tower.

From the Galeries Lafayette, the nearest Métro station is Chaussée d'Antin—La Fayette (lines **7** and **9**).

PIGALLE

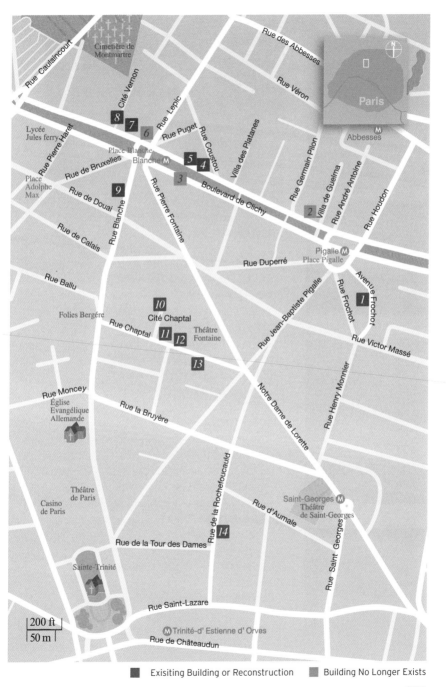

Exisiting Building or Reconstruction   Building No Longer Exists

Cabaret L'Enfer

Boulevard de Clichy

Place Pigalle, c. 1890

START:
Métro at Pigalle

MÉTRO:
2 or 12

END:
Métro
Trinité–d'Estienne d'Orves

MÉTRO:
12

In the late 19th century, the further down the hill of Montmartre one traveled, the more genteel the way of life became, until bohemia blended into the bourgeois elegance of the grands boulevards. The change reflected a transformation that took place as artists, writers and composers who had made a reputation and, in some cases, a fortune, bought homes where they could enjoy their comfort and old age. So many of these artists clustered in the streets below boulevard de Clichy that the area became known as "The New Athens." But once the artists abandoned the studios, bars and cafés of Pigalle and place Blanche, the area was quickly invaded by the demimonde. In the streets where Renoir and Picasso once had their studios, pimps and prostitutes prowled.

Exit the Métro at Pigalle (Line ❷ or ⑫).

Place Pigalle is named for the sculptor Jean-Baptiste Pigalle, who lived from 1714 to 1785. In 1906, Victor Leca's *Secret Guide* to *Parisian Pleasures* called this "the gayest place in Paris, where you can see the nicest girls." On place Pigalle itself, he recommended some establishments "where great *cocottes* [prostitutes] come every night." These included Café de la Nouvelle Athènes, the Abbaye de Thélème (named for the abbey in François Rabelais's *Gargantua* where every pleasure could be satisfied), and the notorious Au Rat Mort (The Dead Rat). Most offered private rooms where *cocottes* could entertain clients. In 1899, Toulouse-Lautrec painted such a scene in his *In a Private Room—At the "Rat Mort,"* also known as *Lucy Jourdan, Private Room No.7*. By World War II, "Pig Alley," as servicemen called it, became synonymous with street prostitution. Although most such activity has migrated downhill, to rue Saint-Denis, Pigalle is notable mainly for its sex shops, strip joints and all-around sleaziness.

Cross to downhill side of Place Pigalle and descend avenue Frochot.

Henri de Toulouse-Lautrec, *Au Rat Mort*, 1899

Café de la Nouvelle Athènes

1 Now one of Paris's many "gated communities," avenue Frochot is the former home of Pierre-Auguste Renoir and his son Jean Renoir, whose 1954 film *French Cancan* celebrated the popularization of the dance by the cabaret owners of Pigalle. Pablo Picasso and Henri de Toulouse-Lautrec also lived here, as did jazz musician Django Reinhardt. More recently, it became popular with people from the worlds of fashion and design; for a while, 2 bis, avenue Frochot was the home of *couturier* Jean Paul Gaultier.

Cabaret du Néant c. 1892

Cabaret L'Enfer c. 1899

Café Cyrano c. 1920

Return to Place Pigalle. Cross to uphill side and continue on boulevard de Clichy.

2 No. 34, boulevard de Clichy is the former site of the Cabaret du Néant (Cabaret of Nothingness), which opened in 1892. In its Salle d'Intoxication, clients sat under chandeliers made of human bones and drank at tables in the form of coffins.

3 The Cabaret L'Enfer (Cabaret of Hell) and Cabaret du Ciel (Cabaret of Heaven), were once located at 53, boulevard de Clichy. The entrance to the former, a gaping mouth with a doorman in a devil costume holding a pitchfork, was one of the infamous sights of Montmartre.

4 The Hôtel and Café Chat Noir, located at 68, boulevard de Clichy, display Théophile Steinlen's famous black cat poster for the Chat Noir. It's not clear they had any connection with the 19th-century cabaret run by Rodolphe Salis on boulevard Rochechouart.

5 The Musée de l'érotisme (72, boulevard de Clichy) is a discreet and well-organized museum devoted to a subject closest to the hearts of this community. In 1997, the seven floors of this former cabaret became a showcase of everything from tribal religious/erotic art to an exhibition on the history of the French *bordel*. Open from 10 a.m. to 2 a.m. **www.musee-erotisme.com**

6 The former site of Brasserie Cyrano (76-78, boulevard de Clichy), was meeting place of the Surrealists from 1925 to the 1950s. Each evening around 5 p.m., the "hour of the aperitif," André Breton strolled across the place from his apartment at 42, rue Fontaine to preside over the evening *séance*.

7 Since 1889, the Moulin Rouge or Red Windmill (82, boulevard de Clichy) has been one of Paris's most recognizable symbols, on a par with the Eiffel Tower, which was completed the same year. It stands on the site of La Reine Blanche, a dance hall dating back to 1850. The new owners put the dancehall in the basement and built a cabaret at street level, topped by the famous red mill. A park at the rear became an open-air theater, dominated by a looming plaster elephant containing private rooms for discreet assignations. The mill itself was purely decorative. "All it ever ground was the customers' money," said Jane Avril, one of its many stars made famous by the paintings of Toulouse-Lautrec, for whom a seat at the Moulin Rouge was permanently reserved. The original buildings burned down in 1924. Promoted as "The First Palace of Women," the original Moulin presented shows exclusively for men, featuring suggestive songs and the notorious *can-can*. The modern Moulin Rouge is an expensive cabaret/restaurant admitting both men and women. It still features the *can-can*. **www.moulinrouge.fr**

Toulouse-Lautrec and Moulin Rouge manager, Mr. Tremolada, 1892

Then & Now

Cabaret L'Enfer c. 1899

Moulin Rouge c. 1898-1911

Edgar Degas

8 Cité Véron is a narrow lane beyond the restaurant to the left of the Moulin Rouge at 92, boulevard de Clichy. Only 262 feet long by 10 feet, it is named for Louis Véron, mayor of Montmartre from 1830 to 1841. It metamorphosed after World War II into a street of lofts and studios. In 1953, poet Jacques Prévert lived at 6b, next door to Boris Vian, novelist, jazz trumpeter, critic and translator (of books including Raymond Chandler's *The Big Sleep*). Vian wrote his song "Le Déserteur" and the novel *L'Arrache-cœur* (*The Heartsnatcher*) here. Novelist Raymond Queneau and playwright Eugène Ionesco also lived here. Today it houses a small theater and dance studios.

Cross Place Blanche to rue Blanche and descend rue Blanche.

9 The Impressionist painter Edgar Degas once lived at 77, rue Blanche.

Turn left onto rue Chaptal.

10 From 1887 to 1962, Cité Chaptal, the converted chapel at 7, rue Chaptal at the end of this lane housed the Grand Guignol, a theater specializing in bloodthirsty plays with such realistic stage effects that patrons often fainted. Since 1976, it has been the International Visual Theatre, devoted to theatrical productions for the deaf and classes in sign language.

11 No. 16, rue Chaptal is the former home of Ary Scheffer, and since 1986 the Musée Renan-Scheffer/Musée de la Vie Romantique. Dutch-born painter Ary Scheffer enjoyed the patronage of Louis-Philippe and the royal family, which made his Friday evening salons a showcase for the artistic

elite. Regular attendees included George Sand, Frédéric Chopin, Eugène Delacroix, Jean-Auguste-Dominique Ingres and Alphonse de Lamartine, as well as visitors Charles Dickens and Ivan Turgenev. His home, studios, greenhouse, garden and grounds have become the setting for an impressive collection of memorabilia and paintings of La Nouvelle Athènes. **www.vie-romantique.paris.fr**

Continue along rue Chaptal and joing rue de la Rochefoucauld. Descend rue de la Rochefoucauld.

🖽 From 1937 to 1948, the building at 14, rue Chaptal housed the Hot Club de France, formed by Pierre Nourry, Charles Delaunay and Hugues Panassié to promote the appreciation of jazz. In 1937, the Club sponsored the formation of the Quintette du Hot Club de France to showcase gypsy guitarist Django Reinhardt and violinist Stéphane Grappelli.

Frédéric Chopin
from a drawing by
George Sand, 1870

13 Offices and storerooms of art dealers Goupil et Cie, for whom Vincent van Gogh and his younger brother Théo worked, were located at 9, rue Chaptal. (Their uncle, also named Vincent, was a partner in the firm.) In 1886, Vincent returned to Paris from London and moved in with Théo. Long nights spent wrangling in local cafés with Camille Pissarro, Claude Monet, Paul Gauguin and Toulouse-Lautrec energized Vincent with the new creed of Impressionism. Shortly after, he moved to Arles in search of more color and light, but suffered the first of his major breakdowns and was hospitalized.

14 A visit to the Musée National Gustave Moreau at 14, rue de la Rochefoucauld can be an eerie experience. Two years before his death in 1896, Moreau, who had taught Georges Rouault and Henri Matisse, demolished his home and studio and commissioned a new building, designed to show off his work to future generations. He planned all its features, including a rotating display of watercolors and a sinuous spiral staircase. The thousands of artworks on show embody a mystical, often sinister sensibility, expressed in his versions of Greek myths and episodes from the Bible. André Breton discovered the museum at age 16, and credited Moreau's flamboyant imagination as an inspiration for Surrealism. **www.musee-moreau.fr**

Continue down rue de la Rochefoucauld to rue Saint-Lazare. Turn right to Métro Trinité—d'Estienne d'Orves (Line **12**).

138. PARIS — Panorama de Montmartre, pris de la terrasse du M
des Galeries Lafayette   C. M.

MONTMARTRE

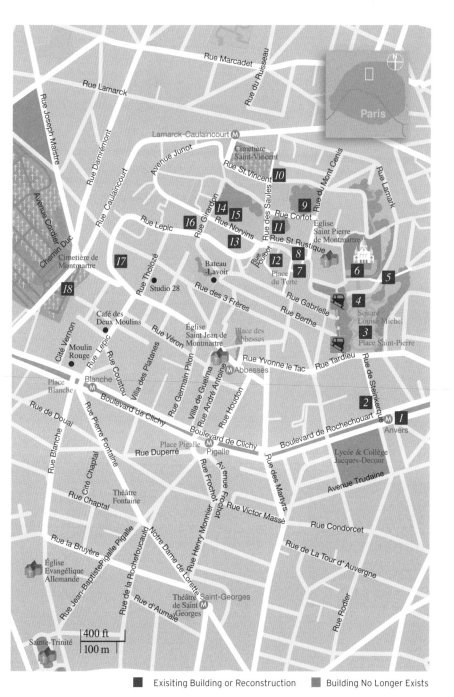

Exisiting Building or Reconstruction   Building No Longer Exists

Moulin de la Galette, circa 1840

Moulin de la Galette, 1880

Place du Tertre, 1924

Originally a village outside the borders of Paris, perched on a sandstone bluff above the city, Montmartre grew into Paris's northernmost suburb, a refuge for political radicals, criminals, performers, prostitutes and artists.

The best time to visit Montmartre depends on the weather, the season and your stamina. Its lanes and staircases are steep. In winter, the wind whips down, making the cobbles icy and treacherous, while in summer they trap the air and heat it like in an oven. From the summit, potential walks radiate in every direction. The following itinerary, which includes the Montmartre Cemetery, is designed to give a taste of this rich district.

If you have time, exit Métro at Barbès–Rochechouart (Lines ②, ④), at the intersection of boulevard Rochechouart and boulevard de Magenta. This noisy intersection with its crowds and the elevated Métro overhead can be daunting, but the noise and confusion decrease as you move uphill. Walk up the righthand side of boulevard de Rochechouart, occupied almost entirely by the clothing and appliances store Tati. Otherwise, begin the tour at Métro station Anvers (Line **2**).

1 Métro station Anvers is a well-preserved example of Hector Guimard's Métro entrances from about 1902. The sinuous cast-iron Art Nouveau pillars and railings, enameled in green, imitate vines and long-stalked flowers, but also suggest ancient bronzes covered in verdigris. Initially these entrances were roundly criticized. The newspaper *Figaro* called them "crooked chandeliers signaling the Métro stops with bulging frog's eyes." However Guimard's system of prefabricated elements assembled on site was so economical that it won over the authorities.

2 Turn right onto rue de Steinkerque. This lane almost defines the term "tourist trap." Dozens of stores overflow with postcards, T-shirts and miscellaneous souvenirs. In the middle of the street, a few dubious characters are usually running the traditional con of three-card monte, deftly shuffling cards or coasters on the improvised table of a cardboard box and inviting the gullible to "spot the lady" and win money.

3 A traditional *manège* or carousel operates on the square at Place Saint-Pierre. (*Manège* means "riding school," which the carousel with its wooden horses resembles.) French children don't reach for a brass ring but for a tassel. The one who grabs it gets a free carousel ride.

Valadon and Utrillo

Take the funicular railway up the hill for the price of a Métro ticket—or, if you have the energy, climb the hundreds of steps running beside it. The sloping square from which the funicular departs is called Place Suzanne Valadon, after the painter, model and mother of Maurice Utrillo.

4 The *terrasse* of the Basilica of Sacré-Cœur offers a sweeping panorama of Paris. It is invariably busy with tourists, as well as street performers—in particular "living statues" and musicians. Among the latter, the jangling zither-like tone of Ecuadorian harpist Hugo Barahona is inextricably associated with the terrace.

Continue along the terrace to the top of rue Maurice Utrillo.

5 Named for one of Montmartre's most famous painters, rue Maurice Utrillo is actually a steep flight of steps. Don't descend unless you have the energy to climb back again to continue your walk.

Ascend the steps to the Basilica of Sacré-Cœur.

6 Begun in 1875 and built on the foundations of a Roman temple, Sacré-Cœur (the Sacred Heart), was intended as a monument to the clergy killed in the Socialist rebellion of the Commune. By the time it was completed in 1919, public sympathy had shifted to the tens of thousands of Communards executed in reprisal, and to the dead of the recent Great War. The interior of the church is architecturally undistinguished. However, the view from the dome (where payment is required to enter) is even more impressive than from the terrace.

Exit Basilica onto Place du Tertre.

7 With its stalls selling postcards and prints and its scores of caricaturists clamoring for clients, café-lined place du Tertre is the very heart of tourist Paris. Pleasant to visit before 10 a.m., it quickly becomes congested. On December 24, 1898, Louis Renault drove one of his cars into the square, proving the capacity of his vehicles to climb the highest hills, and launching the French automobile industry.

8 Chez la Mère Catherine is located at 6, place du Tertre. Russian soldiers occupying Paris in 1814 after the rout and exile of Napoleon demanded food with the word *"bystro,"* the Russian word for "quickly." According to legend, this café was the first to become known as a *bistro*.

Exit onto rue du Mont Cenis, then left on rue Cortot.

9 Situated on the highest point of the butte, the Musée de Montmartre (12, rue Cortot) is reputedly the oldest building to survive from the original village. Dating from 1688, it is built on the foundations of an old abbey. For most of the 19th century, it was rented as artists' studios. Suzanne Valadon and her son Maurice Utrillo worked here, as did as Raoul Dufy and composer Erik Satie. Pierre-Auguste Renoir arrived in 1875 and painted a number of important canvases here, including his masterpiece *Bal du Moulin de la Galette*. The garden here was painted by Renoir in 1876 as *The Garden in the rue Cortot, Montmartre;* the tiny private vineyard continues to produce wine. The building was later the residence of Gustave Charpentier, composer of the opera *Louise*. A descendant, architect Claude Charpentier, acquired the building in 1958 and restored it. Today it is a museum dedicated to the area's cultural history.

Louis Renault, 1898

The Garden in the rue Corot, Montmartre, detail

Exit the museum on rue Cortot and turn right on the rue des Saules, which Cézanne painted.

10 At the corner of rue Saint-Vincent is the Lapin Agile, a café named for the famous rabbit mural painted on its façade by André Gill. At the turn of the 20th century, the café was frequented by Picasso, Modigliani, Utrillo and other struggling artists of the Montmartre scene.

Turn back on rue des Saules and walk to the corner of rue Saint-Rustique.

11 A wall plaque at 18, rue Saint-Rustique, indicates the site of Au Billards de Bois, the former *guinguette* (outdoor wine shop) that Vincent van Gogh painted as *La Guinguette*. From 1900, this was a popular meeting place of Degas, Sisley, Toulouse-Lautrec, Renoir and Monet. Today it's the bistro A La Bonne Franquette.

Continue onto rue Norvins. Turn right onto rue Poulbot. This street is named for artist Francisque Poulbot (1879-1946), famous in France for his sentimental cartoons of big-eyed street kids.

12 Espace Dalí Montmartre is a museum dedicated to the artist Salvador Dalí. The Spanish Surrealist never lived in Montmartre (preferring Montparnasse or, once he became rich, a suite at the Hôtel Meurice), but this gallery boasts 330 pieces by the artist, mostly sculpture, furniture and works in glass, but also etchings for Ovid's *Art of Love*, Lewis Carroll's *Alice in Wonderland*, Cervantes's *Don Quixote* and Rabelais's *Gargantua*. For more information visit **www.daliparis.com**

Return to rue Norvins and turn left.

Then & Now

Lapin Agile, 1927

Moulin de la Galette, 1899

Place du Tertre, 1925

13 In 1914, painter and sculptor Amedeo Modigliani lived at 13, rue Norvins.

14 French writer Marcel Aymé—best known for his short stories—once lived at 26, rue Norvins.

15 Place Marcel Aymé. Here you'll find a sculpture by Jean Marais of man emerging from a wall, inspired by Aymé's story *Le Passe-Muraille* (The Man Who Walked Through Walls).

Continue along rue Norvins and turn left, briefly, down rue Girardon and onto rue Lepic.

16 The Moulin de la Galette is located at 83, rue Lepic on the corner of rue Girardon. The original Moulin de la Galette dates from 1622 and originally stood higher up the butte. From 1809, the Debray family ran a *guinguette* in the yard here, serving products made with its flour—"*galette*" is the loose term for various sorts of baked goods like cakes, breads and even pancakes. As Montmartre became a suburb of Paris, Debray stopped grinding grain, turned the mill into an observation tower and opened a dance hall next door. In the late 19th century, it became a popular venue for parties and dances but fell into disrepair. In 1915, the Friends of Old Montmartre bought it to prevent its demolition. In 1924, the mill was moved to the site and declared a monument in 1939. It was restored in 1978, though it no longer functions. The mill itself and parties held there provided the inspiration for numerous paintings, including Renoir's *Bal du Moulin de la Galette* and works by van Gogh, Pissarro and Picasso.

17 Continue to 54, rue Lepic, where Vincent van Gogh lived with his brother Théo from 1886 until

February 1888, when he left for Arles, leaving nearly 200 canvases behind.

Turn right onto rue Joseph de Maistre and left on rue Caulaincourt. Stay on the left side and walk down the stairs to the entrance of Montmartre Cemetery.

18 Covering 48 acres, Montmartre Cemetery is the final resting place of numerous celebrities, mostly of the 19th century, and the site of some striking monuments. Occupants include authors (Stendahl, Feydeau, Heine); composers (Offenbach, Delibes, Berlioz); artists (Degas, Picabia, Moreau); filmmakers (Truffaut, Clouzot, Autant-Lara); as well as society hostess Juliette Récamier, famously painted by David in 1800, dancer Vaslav Nijinsky and actor Frédéric Lemaître. The remains of Moulin Rouge dancer Louise Weber, better known as La Goulue, were transferred here from Pantin Cemetery. Her gravestone boldly credits her as "*creatrice du French cancan.*" Of special interest are Nijinsky's tomb, with a bronze statue of the dancer in costume for *Petroushka,* and the full-figure bronze by Jules Franceschi on the grave of Polish soldier Miecislas Kamienski, killed at the battle of Magenta in 1859. Adolphe Sax, inventor of the saxophone, is commemorated with a golden example of the instrument. The grave of art critic Jules Castagnary is adorned with a bust by Rodin. Émile Zola was buried here until 1912, when his remains were transferred to the Pantheon, the highest compliment that can be paid to a French citizen; a monument here marks the site of his original grave.

Degas

Exit the Cemetery onto rue Caulaincourt. Continue downhill to boulevard de Clichy and continue to Métro Place de Clichy (lines **2** and **10**).

Zola

LATIN QUARTER & NOTRE DAME

1 Place Saint-Michel
2 Théâtre de la Huchette: 23, rue de la Huchette
3 Le Panier Fleuri: 14, rue de la Huchette
4 Rue du Chat-qui-Pêche
5 Café Chat-qui-Pêche: 10, rue de la Huchette
6 Caveau de la Huchette: 5, rue de la Huchette
7 Church of Saint-Séverin
8 Church of Saint Julien-le-Pauvre
9 Parc René Viviani
10 Shakespeare and Company: 37, rue de la Bûcherie
11 Crypte Archéologique: Place du Parvis-Notre-Dame
12 Notre-Dame de Paris

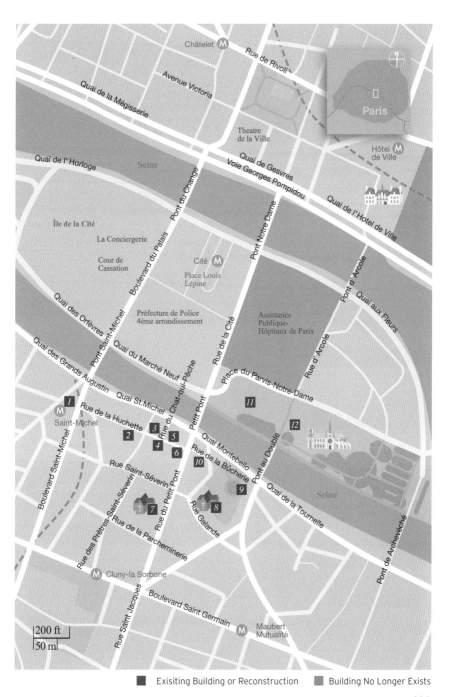

Château

Rue de Rivoli

Avenue Victoria

Quai de la Mégisserie

Theatre
de la Ville

Quai de l' Horloge

Quai de Gesvres

Hôtel
de Ville

Seine

Voie Georges Pompidou

Quai de l'Hotel de Ville

Île de la Cité

La Conciergerie

Cité

Pont d'Arcole

Quai aux Fleurs

Cour de
Cassation

Place Louis
Lépine

Quai des Orfèvres

Préfecture de Police
4ème arrondissement

Assistance
Publique-
Hôpitaux de Paris

Rue d'Arcole

Quai des Grands Augustin

Quai du Marché Neuf

Rue de la Cité

Place du Parvis-Notre-Dame

Quai St.Michel

1

Saint-Michel

Rue de la Huchette

11

3

2

5

4

12

6

Rue de la Bûcherie

10

Boulevard Saint-Michel

Rue Saint-Séverin

9

Rue des Prêtres-Saint-Séverin

7

8

Rue Galande

Rue de la Parcheminerie

Quai de la Tournelle

Seine

Cluny-la Sorbone

Rue Saint Jacques

Boulevard Saint Germain

Pont de l'Archevêché

Maubert
Mutualité

200 ft
50 ml

Existing Building or Reconstruction   Building No Longer Exists

START:
Métro at Saint-Michel

MÉTRO:
4

END:
Métro Hôtel de Ville

MÉTRO:
❶ or 11

View from Notre Dame, 1935

The Joyous Latin Quarter,
1895

Rue de la Huchette, rue de Saint-Séverin and the lanes that connect them are a relic of medieval Paris, much of which was rebuilt in the mid-19th century. Because Latin was the common language of both students and teachers in the religious schools that clustered around the cathedral of Notre Dame, this became known as the *quartier latin* or Latin Quarter. Once the wild behavior of secular students and bohemian artists gave the area a reputation for roguishness, the Latin Quarter became synonymous with cellar nightclubs and showgirls. The present street scene, filled with restaurants and tourist hotels, barely resembles the *quartier latin* of the 1930s and 1940s, when it was the lively community of small tradesmen celebrated by novelist Elliot Paul in *The Last Time I Saw Paris* and *Springtime in Paris*. All the same, relics from all three eras mingle in the modern Latin Quarter in a noisy, crowded *mélange*.

Leave the Métro at Saint-Michel (Line ❹) and take the exit to place Saint-Michel.

1 Place Saint-Michel is dominated by the Fontaine Saint-Michel. Francisque-Joseph Duret's statue of the archangel Michael trampling the devil is flanked by water-spouting dragons by Henri Alfred Jacquemart. Notably, the panel of children and greenery above Michael's head is by a woman artist, Noémie Constant. When the fountain was dedicated in 1860, city planner Baron Georges-Eugène Haussmann asked its architect, Gabriel Davioud, to also design the buildings of the square, creating a spectacular entrance to the newly built boulevard Saint-Michel. After World War II, the fountain was rededicated to French citizens who died resisting Nazi occupation. The square is a famous student hangout and a venue for street entertainers, particularly on weekends.

Cross boulevard Saint-Michel and enter rue de la Huchette.

Saint-Michel c. 1851-70

2 Since 1957, the 85-seat Théâtre de la Huchette (23, rue de la Huchette) has presented only plays by Eugène Ionesco. More than 1.5 million spectators have seen its double bill of *The Lesson* and *The Bald Prima Donna*. **www.theatre-huchette.com**

3 At 14, rue de la Huchette, the "Y" cut into the façade is thought to indicate the former premises of a 15th-century needle-maker. (The letter "Y" in French, called *"y-Greque"*—pronounced "e-grek"—sounds like *"lie-gregues,"* a term for the lacings used to attach stockings to a chemise.) In *The Last Time I Saw Paris,* Elliot Paul preferred a different interpretation and made the address the site of the fictional neighborhood bordello, Le Panier Fleuri (Basket of Flowers).

4 The rue du Chat-qui-Pêche (Street of the Fishing Cat) is one of the narrowest streets in Paris, leading to the quai de Montebello and the Seine, it's probably named for the former premises of a fishmonger. A stone at the corner has the original street name and number of the *arrondissement*.

5 No. 10, rue de la Huchette is now the Café Chat-qui-Pêche. Napoleon Bonaparte lived on the top floor of this building in 1795, near starvation after being suspended for disobeying orders. His fortunes changed in October when he routed a Royalist mob with "a whiff of grapeshot." By March, he was commanding the French Army in Italy.

6 Caveau de la Huchette at 5, rue de la Huchette, is a jazz venue in a medieval cellar where Lionel Hampton, "Memphis Slim," Harry "Sweets" Edison and Art Blakey's Jazz Messengers have performed. Today's music is swing and boogie, suitable for dancing. **www.caveaudelahuchette.fr**

Exit onto rue du Petit Pont. Turn right, then make the first right onto rue Saint-Séverin. Then turn left on rue des Prêtres-Saint-Séverin to enter the Church of Saint-Séverin.

Napoleon Bonaparte

7 Parts of the Gothic church of Saint-Séverin date back to the 13th century, though most of it is from the 15th. A haven of calm in this busiest of neighborhoods, it is notable for its candy-twist columns. Because of the narrowness of the nave, the vaulting rises at so steep an angle that the writer J.-K. Huysmans compared the effect to a grove of palm trees.

Exit the church and turn left, then left onto rue de la Parcheminerie, named for its medieval tenants who scraped sheepskin to make parchment. Turn left again onto rue du Petit Pont.

Approaching from this direction, you will have a better view of the gargoyles along the roofline of the Church of Saint-Séverin.

Return to rue de la Huchette, cross rue du Petit Pont and enter rue Galande.

8 The Church of Saint-Julien-le-Pauvre (Saint Julien the Poor) is located at 79, rue Galande. One of Paris's oldest churches, it dates to 1165 and has been attended by Petrarch, François Rabelais and François Villon. The church has repeatedly been looted, burned and partly rebuilt. Sections of earlier walls are preserved in the forecourt. Used as a wool and wheat storehouse after the 1789 Revolution, it was saved from demolition in 1889 and rededicated as a Greek Orthodox church.

On April 14, 1921, Tristan Tzara, André Breton, Philippe Soupault and Francis Picabia, among others, stood outside the church and heckled passersby with rude comments—"He should trim his nose as one trims his hair!"—and offered fake guided tours that included a visit to the morgue. This "Dada Excursion" was regarded as a failure and the event further widened the rift between Tzara and Breton. Shortly after, Breton and his followers broke away to launch Surrealism.

Saint-Julien, 1898

To the right of the church, on the malodorous site of a former well, a stone slab is all that remains of the Roman Road, a 4th-century highway that ran south along rue Saint-Jacques.

Tristan Tzara reading to the crowd, 1921

Parc René Viviani, 1935

9 Stonework and statuary removed from Notre Dame during its mid-19th century restoration is scattered around Parc René Viviani, an attractive little park that contains Paris's oldest living tree, a plugged and buttressed *Robinia pseudoacacia* or False Acacia. Jean Robin, herbalist to Henry IV, imported seeds from North America in 1601. This example dates from 1680.

Continue to the riverbank and turn left.

10 The famous Shakespeare and Company bookshop—a literary landmark specializing in English-language books—stands at 37, rue de la Bûcherie. On the death of Sylvia Beach, founder of the original Shakespeare and Company, bookseller George Whitman, proprietor of the Mistral Bookshop, acquired its lending library and, in 1964, its name. It became a famous watering hole for visiting writers, in particular "Beats" like Gregory Corso, Allen Ginsberg and Gary Snyder. Books from Beach's library furnish the first floor, a venue for readings and writing classes. The rare book room to the left of the main entrance is open only by appointment. **www.shakespeareandcompany.com**

Cross the Petit Pont bridge to the Île de le Cité and place du Parvis-Notre-Dame.

11 Under the *parvis* or forecourt of Notre-Dame Cathedral, the Crypte Archéologique/Archeological Crypt is a museum that exposes the foundations of the city, including a Celtic settlement of the Iron Age and stonework from Roman Paris dating back to about 50 BCE.

12 Notre-Dame de Paris is one of the most imposing sights of Paris, and among the most visited. Completed in 1345, the cathedral took two centuries to build, and has been extensively defaced and restored ever since. Among the great events that took place here are the coronation of King Henry VI of England in 1431, the crowning of Napoleon (by himself) as emperor in 1804, the canonization of Joan of Arc in 1920, the celebration of the liberation of Paris in 1944 (interrupted by sniper fire), and the 1970 requiem mass for Charles de Gaulle.

The 28 statues above the main portal show the biblical kings of Judah, but revolutionaries beheaded them in 1793, believing they represented kings of France. Architect Eugène Viollet-le-Duc had them replaced during the massive restoration that began in 1845. (The heads were later found buried behind the Abbey of Cluny in 1977, and are on display in the Musée Cluny.)

Arrival of the Emperor Napoleon, August 15, 1807

If you can manage 255 steps and don't mind waiting in line, the top of the North Tower offers a view of the famous gargoyles in the Gallery of Chimeras added by Viollet-le-Duc and statues of the apostles, plus one of Viollet-le-Duc himself. (The saints look out over Paris; the architect looks inwards, admiring his work.) For an even better view of the

Joan of Arc in Notre Dame

Notre Dame, 1827

View from Notre Dame

Viollet-le-Duc looks inward

Cathedral Interior,
c. 1890-1900

city, ascend an additional 125 steps to the summit of the South Tower, which also houses the 13-ton Emmanuel, the largest of the cathedral's five bells. They are tolled infrequently, since their vibration could damage the building's structure.

Stepping inside, the first thing one notices about Notre Dame is its awe-inspiring size. The building is 427 feet long by 157 feet wide and can seat 9,000. The highest vault is 115 feet above the floor. Only the North and South windows are original; as part of an 18th-century "modernization," Louis XIV and Louis XV replaced the rest with clear glass. Most of the present colored windows date from after WWII.

Though most wooden features of the cathedral were burned during the Revolution and the Commune, the carved choir stalls are preserved. On the north side of the chancel, a 14th-century relief depicts the life of Christ. In marble, the most distinguished work is the *Pietà* by 18th-century sculptor Nicolas Coustou, behind the Choir Altar.

Located to the side of the choir, near the front of the cathedral, the Treasury houses a reliquary designed by Viollet-le-Duc to hold a nail from Christ's crucifixion, a fragment of wood from the cross and a thorn from the Crown of Thorns. Also on display are manuscripts, crosses, chalices and Napoleon's coronation robes.

For more information on Paris's famous cathedral visit **www.notredamedeparis.fr**

Exit Notre-Dame de Paris and turn right on rue d'Arcole. Continue to Pont d'Arcole and cross the Seine to Métro Hôtel de Ville (lines ① and ⑪).

French writers of the nineteenth century

SAINT-GERMAIN-DES-PRÉS & ODÉON

1. Church of Saint-Germain-des-Prés
2. Square Laurent-Prache: 3, place Saint-Germain-des-Prés
3. Sartre Apartment: 42, rue Bonaparte
4. *Prométhée*
5. Wallace Fountain
6. Café aux Deux Magots: 6, place Saint-Germain-des-Prés
7. Café de Flore: 172, boulevard Saint-Germain
8. Brasserie Lipp: 151, boulevard Saint-Germain
9. Place du Québec
10. Place Saint-Sulpice
11. Church of Saint-Sulpice
12. Café de la Marie: 8, place St-Sulpice
13. Fitzgerald Apartment: 58, rue Vaugirard

14. Hôtel de Luzy: 6, rue Ferou
15. Man Ray Studio: 2 bis, rue Ferou
16. Musée du Luxembourg
17. Grand Hôtel des Principautes-Unies: 42, rue Vaugirard
18. Café Tournon: 18, rue Tournon
19. Théâtre de l'Odéon: 2, rue Corneille
20. Café Voltaire: 1, place de l'Odéon
21. Restaurant la Méditerranée: 2, place de l'Odéon
22. Beach/Monnier Apartment: 18, rue de l'Odéon
23. Paine Apartment: 16, rue de l'Odéon
24. Former Location of Shakespeare and Company: 12, rue de l'Odéon
25. Maison des Amis des Livres: 7, rue de l'Odéon
26. Contact Editions: 8, rue de l'Odéon

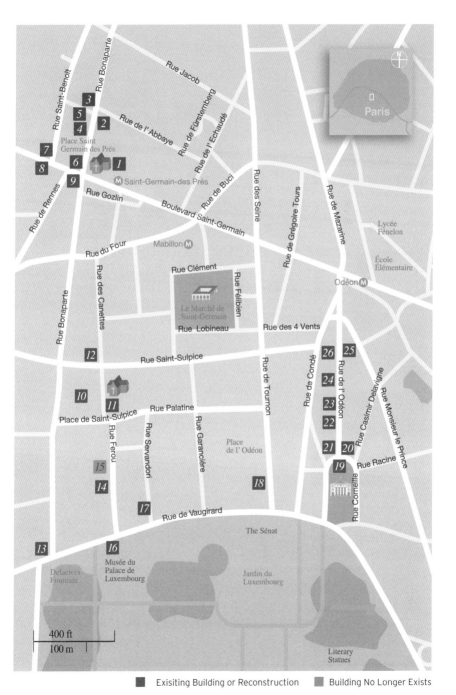

N

Paris

Rue Jacob

Rue Saint-Benoît

Rue Bonaparte

Rue de Fürstenberg

3

5

4

2

Rue de l'Abbaye

Rue de l' Echaudé

7

Place Saint
Germain des Prés

6

1

8

9

Rue Gozlin

Saint-Germain-des-Prés

Rue de Buci

Rue des Seine

Boulevard Saint-Germain

Rue de Grégoire Tours

Rue de Mazarine

Lycée
Fénelon

École
Élémentaire

Rue de Rennes

Rue du Four

Mabillon

Odéon

Rue Bonaparte

Rue des Canettes

Rue Clément

Rue Félibien

Le Marché de
Saint-Germain

Rue Lobineau

Rue des 4 Vents

12

Rue Saint-Sulpice

Rue de Tournon

Rue de Condé

26 25

24

23

22

21 20

Rue de l' Odéon

Rue Casimir Delavigne

Rue Monsieur le Prince

10

11

Place de Saint-Sulpice

Rue Palatine

Rue Ferou

Rue Servandoni

Rue Garancière

Place
de l' Odéon

18

19

Rue Racine

Rue Corneille

15

14

17

Rue de Vaugirard

13

16

Musée du
Palace de
Luxembourg

Delacroix
Fountain

The Sénat

Jardin du
Luxembourg

Literary
Statues

400 ft

100 m

Exisiting Building or Reconstruction ■   Building No Longer Exists ■

START:
Métro at Saint-Germain-des-Prés

MÉTRO:
④

END:
Métro at Odéon

MÉTRO:
④ or ⑩

René Descartes

Boulvard Saint-Germain

The district of Saint-Germain-des-Prés is centered on the church of the same name. The name means literally "Saint Germain in the fields," since for more than two centuries the abbey to which the church belonged stood outside the city walls. After World War II, the area became synonymous with philosophy, jazz and the French equivalent of the Beat Generation.

Exit Métro at Saint-Germain-des-Prés (Line ④) on north side of boulevard Saint-Germain, nearest the church.

1 Parts of the church of Saint-Germain-des-Prés date from 1542, but centuries of plundering and restoration have left a muddle of medieval Romanesque and Gothic elements capped by a 19th-century spire. The neo-Classical murals are by Jean-Hippolyte Flandrin, a pupil of Ingres. The heart of philosopher René Descartes is interred here, though the rest of his body has been moved to the Pantheon.

2 Next to the church, stone arches in the tiny Square Laurent-Prache park are all that remain of the 13th-century Chapel of the Virgin. The space was dedicated in 1969 to poet Guillaume Apollinaire. Puzzlingly, Pablo Picasso contributed a bronze head of one-time mistress Dora Maar, whom Apollinaire never met. It is nevertheless displayed on a plinth at the gate.

Walk across Place Saint-Germain to the corner of rue Bonaparte.

3 From 1946, Jean-Paul Sartre and his mother Anne-Marie shared an apartment on the corner of Place Saint-Germain at 42, rue Bonaparte. They moved to Montparnasse after the building was bombed in 1961 and 1962 by terrorists angered by Sartre's support of Algerian independence.

Jean-Paul Sartre

Continue toward boulevard Saint-Germain.

4 The 1956 bronze sculpture *Prométhée* by Ossip Zadkine depicts Prometheus, a Titan who stole fire from the gods and gave it to the mortals.

5 Responding to the water shortage that followed the Prussian siege of 1870, British philanthropist and Francophile Sir Richard Wallace commissioned Charles-Auguste Lebourg to design a water fountain and installed 50 of them around Paris. Today there are 67. Originally, a metal cup was chained to each fountain, but these were removed in 1952, after being deemed unhygienic. The supporting female figures represent Kindness, Simplicity, Charity and Sobriety.

Simone de Beauvoir at the Café de Flore

6 At the famous Café aux Deux Magots, two figures of Chinese gentlemen or *magots* survive from its origin in 1813 as a shop for oriental silks, porcelain and tea. From selling tea, the owners began brewing it and reopened as a café around 1881. In the 1940s, it became a rendezvous for the Existentialist followers of Jean-Paul Sartre. The intersection of boulevard Saint-Germain, rue de Rennes and rue Bonaparte is officially Place Jean-Paul Sartre-Simone de Beauvoir.

Continue along boulevard Saint-Germain.

7 Located at 172, boulevard Saint-Germain, Café de Flore gets its name for the statue of Flora, Roman goddess of flowers, that stands by the front door. During World War I, Guillaume Apollinaire, who coined the term "surreal," introduced André Breton to Philippe Soupault, an early ally in creating Surrealism. An upstairs room, formerly the apartment of fascist anti-Semitic writer Charles Maurras, allowed writers to retreat and work, particularly during the Occupation, when Nazi officers co-opted the street level. Simone de Beauvoir wrote *Le Sang des Autres* (*The Blood of Others*) here, and Sartre composed *Les Chemins de la Liberté* (The Roads to Freedom). "Flore was like home to us," said Sartre.

Cross boulevard Saint-Germain.

8 From 1880, Alsatian brewer Léonard Lipp brewed beer in the cellar and served it in the café, called the Brasserie Lipp. The *brasserie*, which means "brewery," is located at 151, boulevard Saint-Germain and still retains the bare board floors and original brass and mirrors. Ernest Hemingway came here for a cheap lunch of hot *cervelas* sausage on cold sliced potatoes dressed with olive oil, and a goblet of Lipp beer. After World War II, Lipp was invaded by editors and writers from nearby publishing houses and prices rose. The glassed-in terrace, the shop-window of the restaurant, is traditionally reserved for movie stars and winners of the Prix Goncourt literary prize.

Cross rue de Rennes to corner of rue Bonaparte.

9 The paved area at this intersection was renamed Place du Québec in 1980. The fountain of water bursting through the paving stones, a gift from the province, was created by architect Alfred Gindre and sculptor Charles Daudelin. The title, *Embâcle*, evokes the breaking up of ice on a frozen river.

Brasserie Lipp c. 1920

Continue down rue Bonaparte—a street known for expensive fashion boutiques and *pâtisseries*—to Place Saint-Sulpice.

10 Place Saint-Sulpice, flanked by the church of Saint-Sulpice and the *mairie* or town hall of the 6th arrondissement, is an impressive public space in a city famous for them. The fountain by Joachim Visconti incorporates statues of four bishops: Bossuet, Fénelon, Fléchier and Massillon. All noted for their learning, none attained the rank of cardinal. They now face north, south, east and west— the cardinal points— and the fountain is known as *La Fontaine des quatre points cardinaux* (which can be read as "The Fountain of the Four Not-Cardinals").

11 Dating from 1754, the Église Saint-Sulpice is the Notre-Dame of the Left Bank and only slightly smaller, although its Romanesque theatricality contrasts with the Gothic drama of its sister on the Île Saint-Louis. If the two-level façade with its

Mural by Eugène Delacroix

Scott and Zelda Fitzgerald

14, rue Guynemer

unfinished south tower resembles a stage set, credit its architect Giovanni Niccolò Servandoni, who mostly designed décor for the royal opera and state weddings. The interior is just as theatrical, with a massive organ and holy water fonts made from the shells of giant clams. The Chapel of the Holy Angels, on the right as you enter, contains murals by Eugène Delacroix, completed in 1861. In 2003, Saint-Sulpice achieved notoriety when Dan Brown included an imaginary hidden passage in his bestseller *The Da Vinci Code*.

12 Henry Miller wrote in *Tropic of Cancer* of sitting at the Café de la Mairie (6, place Saint-Sulpice) and enjoying the "fat belfries" of the church. Hemingway, Fitzgerald and Faulkner all ate here, as did Saul Bellow. Djuna Barnes wrote part of her 1936 novel *Nightwood* here, and mentions it in the text.

Walk across Place Saint-Sulpice and continue up rue Bonaparte.

13 In April 1928, Scott and Zelda Fitzgerald and their daughter Scottie spent five months in a fourth-floor apartment at 58, rue Vaugirard. Scott wrote stories for American magazines while Zelda, increasingly hysterical, studied ballet with Madame Lubov Egorova. Their rich friends Gerald and Sara Murphy had just bought an apartment nearby at 14, rue Guynemer, a strikingly modern Art Deco building by Michel Roux-Spitz. The Murphys may have inspired the characters of Dick and Nicole Diver in *Tender is the Night,* though they are essentially self-portraits of Scott and Zelda.

Turn left on rue Vaugirard, then left onto rue Ferou. In Alexandre Dumas's famous novel, one of the three musketeers, Athos, lived on this narrow street; his friend Aramis lived on rue Servandoni.

14 From late 1927 to the beginning of 1930, Ernest Hemingway lived with his second wife, Pauline Pfeiffer, in a sprawling apartment paid for by her rich uncle, located at 6, rue Ferou, behind a gate flanked by stone sphinxes. Here he worked on *A Farewell to Arms*. The apartment was in the 18th-century Hôtel de Luzy ("Hôtel" in this sense means "residence" or "townhouse"). Returning late and drunk from a night out with poet Archibald MacLeish, Hemingway yanked the wrong chain in the toilet and pulled down a skylight on his head. The gash in his forehead required stitches and he wore his bandages with the arrogance of someone displaying a war wound. The building now belongs to film star Johnny Depp.

15 No. 2 bis, rue Ferou is the former site of Man Ray's post-war studio. After wartime exile in Los Angeles, Ray returned to Paris with his new wife Juliet. From 1951 until his death in 1976, he lived and worked here.

Visitors included Duchamp, Giacometti, Breton, Éluard, Dalí and Buñuel. Juliet stayed until 1983, hoping to restore the decaying building as a museum. The Centre Pompidou acquired the contents before it was demolished in 1989.

Return to rue Vaugirard.

16 Before the national collection of modern art was consolidated in the Centre Pompidou, the small Musée du Luxembourg housed paintings by Paul Cézanne. Hemingway, who aimed to write with the simplicity and directness of Cézanne, paid frequent visits (though it's probably not true that—as he claimed—in hard times, he trapped pigeons in the gardens for his dinner).

Saint-Sulpice seen from rue Ferou, 1898

Ernest and Pauline, c. 1927

William Faulkner

The Sénat

17 Now the Hôtel Luxembourg Parc, the building at 42, rue Vaugirard was formerly the Grand Hôtel des Principautes-Unies, where William Faulkner lived for five months in 1925. He intended to stay longer in Paris, but became disillusioned with the city and returned to America, having realized that "my own little postage stamp of native soil was worth writing about and that I would never live long enough to exhaust it." But the bleak evocation of the Luxembourg Gardens that ends his novel *Sanctuary* shows the visit was not wasted.

Continue on rue Vaugirard to rue de Tournon. The building opposite, now used by the Sénat, was formerly the palace of Marie de Médicis, widow of Henry IV. It copies the Pitti Palace in her native Florence, and its grounds now form part of the Luxembourg Gardens. During World War II, it was the local headquarters of the German air force, the Luftwaffe.

18 Café Tournon is cheaper and quieter than the cafés of boulevard Saint-Germain, which accounts for its popularity with writers. A plaque notes that novelist Joseph Roth lived upstairs in the 1930s. After the war, Scottish writer Alexander Trocchi edited the magazine *Merlin* from here, followed in 1953 by the *Paris Review* of Peter Matthiessen and George Plimpton. Tournon is most famous as a meeting place for the African-American writers of the late '50s, including James Baldwin, Richard Wright and Chester Himes.

Return to rue Vaugirard, continue across rear of Théâtre de l'Odéon, turn left onto rue Corneille, and descend into place de l'Odéon.

19 A theater has occupied this site since the time

of Marie Antoinette, but the present Théâtre de l' Odéon, with its imposing columned portico, is the work of Pierre Thomas Baraguay and dates from 1819. Now known as the Odéon-Théâtre de l'Europe, it is one of the six national theaters and specializes in subtitled presentations of plays performed in languages other than French. In May 1968, then-director Jean-Louis Barrault surrendered the theater to rioting students, who wrecked it.

Cross to the northern (downhill) side of Place de l'Odéon.

20 The Café Voltaire was once located at 1, place de l'Odéon. Opened in 1750, it was patronized by

Meeting at Café Voltaire, 1898

Then & Now

View of the facade of Luxembourg, 1700s

First draft of the théâtre de l'Odéon, 1786

Sylvia Beach and Adrienne
Monnier

Thomas Paine

revolutionaries like Camille Desmoulins, and later
by Balzac, Gauguin and Mallarmé. Playwrights
often waited here to watch the reactions of
audiences as they left the theater.

21 Opened in 1942, the Restaurant la Méditerranée
(2, place de l'Odéon) became a favorite of literary,
film and theater people (Orson Welles, Charlie
Chaplin), and the occasional crowned head
(Princess Margaret). Jean Cocteau designed the
logo that appears on the blue awning and also the
sketch used on its china and linen. Original murals
by Christian Bérard and Marcel Vertes decorate the
walls, as do lithographs by Picasso and Cocteau.

Descend rue de l'Odéon.

22 Sylvia Beach (see **24**), and Adrienne Monnier
(see **25**), shared an apartment on the fourth floor
of the building at 18, rue de l'Odéon from 1920 to
1936. They were visited by most of the important
literary figures of the time, in particular Ernest
Hemingway, Scott Fitzgerald and James Joyce.
When Fitzgerald met Joyce for the first time at a
1929 dinner party here, he fell on his knees before
him. Hemingway's description of "liberating" the
building in 1944 and being embraced by Beach is
largely fabricated. She had moved out in 1936.

23 In 1797, printer Nicholas Bonneville lent a
room to the political writer Thomas Paine at No. 16
(formerly No. 10), rue de l'Odéon. He lived here
until 1802.

24 From 1921 to 1944 Sylvia Beach's Shakespeare
and Company was located at 12, rue de l'Odéon.
Beach first opened the bookstore on nearby rue
Dupyteren but moved this site, closer to her lover

and fellow bookseller Adrienne Monnier. As well as selling and lending English-language books, Beach published *Ulysses,* a generous gesture towards the avaricious James Joyce that left her near bankruptcy. Various expatriates used the one-bedroom apartment above the shop, including, from 1923, avant-garde composer George Antheil. Beach moved there after breaking up with Monnier in 1936. During World War II, it briefly sheltered Samuel Beckett from the Gestapo. The shop closed during the Occupation; Beach reopened it symbolically in 1944, but she was too ill to continue running it. The stock was acquired by George Whitman of the Mistral Bookshop and on her death in 1962, Beach "bequeathed" him the "Shakespeare and Company" name.

Shakespeare and Company

25 From 1915 to 1951, 7, rue de l'Odéon was the site of Adrienne Monnier's Maison des Amis des Livres. As well as selling books, Monnier published them, edited the influential magazines *Le Navire d'Argent*, *Mesures* and *Commerce,* and held readings, including excerpts from Valery Larbaud's French translation of *Ulysses*.

26 No. 8, rue de l'Odéon was once home of author/ publisher Robert McAlmon and, from 1923 to 1929, of his Contact Editions, which published Hemingway's first book *Three Stories and Ten Poems*, as well as works by William Carlos Williams, Gertrude Stein and McAlmon's wife Winifred Ellerman, under the pseudonym "Bryher." Ellerman financed Contact in return for freedom to pursue a lesbian lifestyle, a fact that earned McAlmon the nickname "McAlimony."

View of rue de l'Odéon, 1932

At the end of the street, arrive at the Carrefour de l'Odéon and the Odéon Métro stop (Lines ❹ and ❿).

THE LUXEMBOURG GARDENS

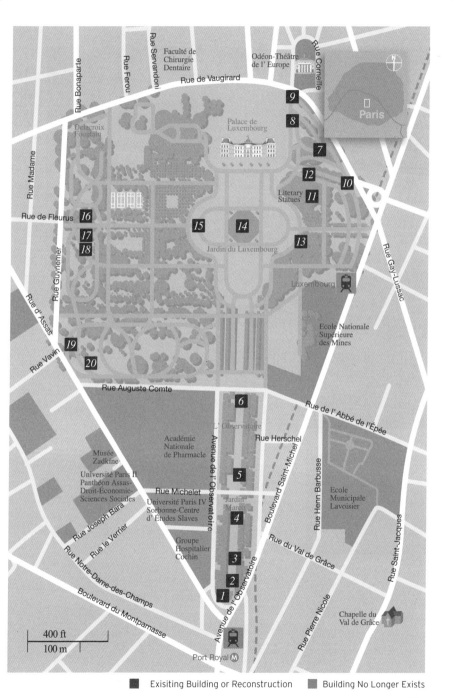

Existing Building or Reconstruction   Building No Longer Exists

START:
RER Station Port-Royal

MÉTRO:
(RER)

END:
RER Station Port-Royal

MÉTRO:
(RER)

Jardin du Luxembourg, c. 1928

Marie de Médicis

Palazzo Pitti, c. 1860

The Jardin du Luxembourg, Paris's second-largest public park, attempts to be all things to all people, and it largely succeeds. Alongside 500 years of history, it offers modern facilities for tennis, *boules* and chess, as well as concerts, cafés, a puppet theater, pony rides, playgrounds, a bee farm, an orchard, and the city's best-maintained flower beds and lawns.

The park is named for the Duke of Luxembourg, from whom Marie de Médicis, widow of Henry IV, bought the land in 1615, though it would be more accurate to call them the Gardens of Florence, since Marie, pining for her native city, ordered Salomon de Brosse to design a palace like Florence's Palazzo Pitti. Tommaso Francini created an Italianate garden of nearly 50 acres bounded by 2,000 elm trees, and featuring a Renaissance fountain, terraces with balustrades and a pond. Ironically, Marie never lived here; her son Louis XIII exiled her after discovering she was plotting against him.

Neglected, the overgrown gardens inspired some of Jean-Antoine Watteau's most charming scenes of carefree court life. After the Revolution, the ruling Directorate seized the land to create a public park. During Haussmann's mid-19th-century reconstruction of Paris, his director of parks, Gabriel Davioud, added ornamental gates and fences and some brick garden houses. A new *allée* or path opened a view of the Pantheon. In 1865, an extension to rue de l'Abbé de l'Epée (now rue Auguste-Comte) severed the upper half of the gardens, creating the Jardin Cavelier Robert de la Salle and the Jardin Marco Polo. Though not technically part of the main park, they are called the "Little Luxembourg."

Exit Métro at Port-Royal (ⓇⒺⓇ Ⓑ). Cross Place Camille-Jullian to the top of Jardin Marco Polo.

Jardin du Luxembourg, 1817

Jardin du Luxembourg, 1840

1 The Fontaine des Quatre-Parties-du-Monde (Fountain of the Four Parts of the World) was commissioned by Baron Georges-Eugène Haussmann and built between 1867-1874. The fountain was designed by Gabriel Davioud, with horses and dolphins by Emmanuel Fremiet. Its centerpiece, *Les Quatre Parties du monde soutenant la sphére céleste* (*Four Parts of the World Supporting a Celestial Sphere*) is by Jean-Baptiste Carpeaux. Figures representing Europe, Africa, Asia and America surround Pierre Legrain's sphere carved with signs of the zodiac. In a reference to emancipation, America stands on the broken chains of the slave trade, wrapped around Africa's ankle.

Descend Jardin Marco Polo. The statues in the Little Luxembourg supposedly represent aspects of day or night, though the symbolism is often obscure.

2 The first statue, *L'Aurore* (*Dawn*), is by François Jouffroy.

3 Jean-Joseph Perraud's *Le Jour* (*Day*) shows a warrior, having laid down his axe but holding onto a horn and with a stone in his sling, being refreshed by a woman with a jug of water. A more appropriate title may be *Midi* (*Noon*).

Cross rue Michelet and enter Jardin Cavelier Robert de la Salle. The park is named for René-Robert Cavelier, Sieur de La Salle, 17th-century explorer of North America.

4 *Le Crépuscule* (*Twilight*) by Gustave Grauk.

5 *La Nuit* (*Night*) by Charles Alphonse Achille Gumery. A male, perhaps Apollo, the sun god, succumbs to the lure of the night as his suspicious hound looks on.

Cross rue Auguste-Comte and enter main Luxembourg Gardens.

The Luxembourg is as much show as garden. Flowerbeds are renewed three times a year with new plants slotted into place after the soil has been injected with steam to kill weeds. Fresh turf is unrolled like carpet. Boxed orange trees, date palms, pomegranates and oleanders are trundled into place like décor in a stage production, and returned to shelter as autumn comes. The distinctive green metal chairs have not changed in a century.

6 This angle offers the best view of the south façade of the Palais de Luxembourg, added between 1836 and 1841 by Alphonse de Gisors.

The building was a prison during the Revolution, and Luftwaffe headquarters during World War II, after which it hosted the 1946 peace conference. It now houses the Sénat or French Senate. Many of Marie de Médicis's original decorations have been restored, although the canvases by Peter Paul Rubens illustrating her life as regent now hang in the Louvre. Except for occasional tours on Jours de Patrimoine, there is no public access.

Descend to lower level and take right-hand path.

Palais Luxembourg, 1750

7 The original Medici Fountain stood against an old orangerie in the middle of what is now avenue du Medicis. By the mid-19th century, only the grotto-like wall remained. In 1864, Alphonse de Gisors moved it to its present location. For support, he placed it back to back with the Fontaine de Léda and added two figures pouring water from stone jars to represent the rivers Rhone and Seine. He restored the Medici coat of arms, which had been defaced during the Revolution, and placed a faun and a huntress in the niches, plus masks representing comedy and tragedy. Auguste Ottin provided a bronze of the giant Polyphemus discovering the lovers Acis and Galatea in marble. With the addition of a tree-shaded pool, they completed the fountain as it is today.

Continue towards exit onto rue de Médicis.

8 Gaston Watkin's monument to French students in the wartime resistance was erected in 1956.

Medici Fountain, 1786

Henri-Désiré Landru

9 A bust by Henri-Théophile Bouillon honors Henry Murger, author of *Scènes de la vie de bohème*, the inspiration for Puccini's *La Bohème*.

Exit onto rue de Médicis and turn right.

The Surrealist Philippe Soupault wrote of the railings here in 1928: "It is said that along one side of it is the meeting place of masochistic bachelors. A modest and silent club. Their umbrellas take on the appearance of a flock."

In 2000, a free exhibition of aerial photographs by Yann-Arthus Bertrand hung on the railings and drew unprecedented crowds. Since then, photo shows have been a feature here.

Re-enter Luxembourg Gardens at the first entrance.

10 Eugène-Louis Lequesne's statue features a faun, or forest god, dancing. Under his feet is the skin of an animal, adapted to hold wine.

11 Visiting bands and choirs frequently perform on the bandstand for patrons of the outdoor café. Serial murderer Henri-Désiré Landru, the original "Bluebeard," met his victims here. Widows lured by his advertisement: "Widower with two children, aged 43, with comfortable income, serious and moving in good society, desires to meet widow with a view to matrimony." Between 1915 and 1919, he murdered 11 people. He was guillotined in 1921.

Continue to steps at the top of the terrace.

12 Arthur Bourgeois' bronze sculpture *The Greek Actor* depicts a young actor, mask on the back of his head and manuscript in hand, learning his lines.

Luxembourg Gardens, 1829

13 Twenty statues of "Queens of France and Illustrious Women" line the terraces on both sides. Dating from the 1840s and the revival of the monarchy, almost all represent real-life queens, nobles or saints. The exception is Clémence Isaure by Antoine-Augustin Préault, the statue of a woman slouching seductively against a column, left arm raised. She is the supposed founder of the Toulouse Flower Festival in the late Middle Ages—and, unlike the other 19 figures, is mythical.

Descend the terrace and cross the central garden to the *bassin* or pond. Throughout the 1920s and 1930s, Gertrude Stein walked here every day from her home on rue de Fleurus. A hungry Ernest Hemingway took the same path when he came from Montparnasse to visit her; the park air wasn't tainted with the tantalising scents of food.

14 The *bassin* is mentioned in *Sanctuary*, by William Faulkner, who lived nearby in 1925. In *The Ambassadors*, Henry James describes his leading character, Lambert Strether, sitting here, visualizing Paris as a "vast bright Babylon, like some huge iridescent object, a jewel brilliant and hard."

The Bassin, 1913

Ascend steps to the upper terrace.

15 The statues lining this terrace are (right to left as seen from the bassin): Sainte Clotilde, Marguerite de Provence, Anne de Bretagne, Anne d'Autriche, Blanche de Castille, Anne de Beaujeu, Valentine de Milan, Marguerite de Valois, Marie de Médicis and Laure de Noyes.

From the steps, a wide *allée* leads to the exit onto rue Guynemer. To the right are tennis courts, a puppet theater and an outdoor café. To the left are

x

public toilets (payment required) and the rear of an orangerie and the Musée du Luxembourg.

Continue to gardens running along rue Guynemer. (As this is a popular jogging track, expect runners, particularly in the morning.) Enter gardens on left of entrance.

16 This 10-foot bronze replica of the Statue of Liberty was donated in 1906 by its sculptor, Auguste Bartholdi. It is shaded by an American oak.

17 Monument to Édouard Branly, radio communications pioneer, by Charles Marie Louis Joseph Sarrabezolles.

18 Monument to composer Jules Massenet, best remembered today for his opera *Manon*. The bleak obelisk was completed by Paul Gasq after designer Raoul Verlet died in 1923.

19 The Pavilion Davioud (formerly the Buffet de la Pépinière) was designed by Gabriel Davioud in 1867 as a café. Today it's home to the École d'horticulture du Luxembourg, a horticultural school.

20 The Rucher école du Jardin du Luxembourg is the park's beekeeping school. The school maintains 12 hives and offers classes in beekeeping.

Exit onto rue Guynemer. Turn left, join rue d'Assas, and ascend to Métro Port-Royal (ⓇⒺⓇ Ⓑ).

MONTPARNASSE

1 La Rotonde: 105, boulevard du Montparnasse
2 Statue of Honoré de Balzac
3 Café Select: 99, boulevard du Montparnasse
4 La Coupole: 102, boulevard du Montparnasse
5 Le Dôme: 108, boulevard du Montparnasse
6 Foujita Studo: 5, rue Delambre
7 *The New Review*: 8, rue Delambre
8 Duncan Apartment: 9, rue Delambre
9 Le Dingo: 10, rue Delambre
10 Rosebud Bar: 11 bis, rue Delambre
11 Man Ray Studio: 13, rue Delambre
12 Grand Hôtel des Écoles: 15, rue Delambre
13 Hôtel des Bains: 33, rue Delambre

14 Hôtel Delambre (Hôtel des Écoles): 35, rue Delambre
15 Le Sphinx: 31, boulevard Edgar Quinet
16 Monocle: 14, boulevard Edgar Quinet
17 Montparnasse Cemetery
18 Hôtel L'Aiglon: 232, boulevard Raspail
19 Man Ray Studio: 31 bis, rue Campagne-Première
20 Hôtel Istria: 29, rue Campagne-Première
21 Passage d'Enfer
22 Atelier 17: 17, rue Campagne-Première
23 Cité des Artistes: 9, rue Campagne-Première
24 Le Jockey: 146, boulevard du Montparnasse
25 Closerie des Lilas: 171, boulevard du Montparnasse

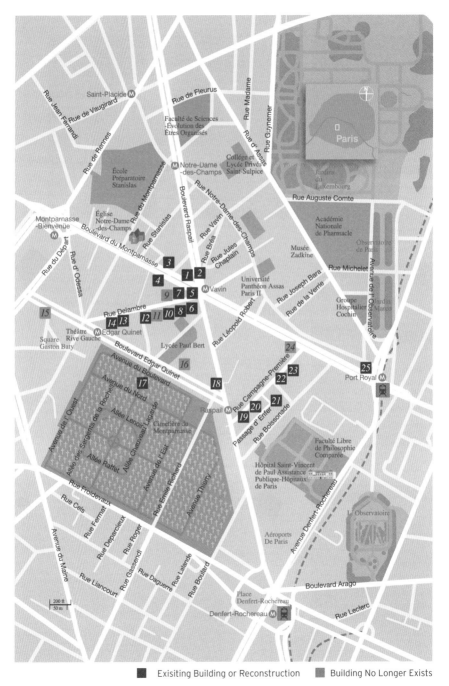

◼ Exisiting Building or Reconstruction   ◼ Building No Longer Exists

START:
Métro at Vavin

MÉTRO:
4

END:
RER Station Port-Royal

MÉTRO:
RER

Le Dôme

Montparnasse is named for Mount Parnassus, the Greek mountain on which the gods were said to have lived. Originally settled by Italian sculptors who executed the stonework for Baron Georges-Eugène Haussmann's rebuilt Paris in the 1850s, it became famous for the number of artists who made it their home. Heavy-drinking painters and promiscuous models gave it a reputation for bohemianism. This persisted well after the artists and models had moved on, encouraged by the bar and café owners who catered to the tourists who flocked there in the 1920s, and continue to do so today.

Exit the Métro at Vavin (Line ❹) at the intersection of boulevard du Montparnasse and boulevard Raspail.

1 On the corner nearest the Métro exit, La Rotonde, opened in 1910, is one of the most famous Paris cafés, patronized by expatriates of every

nationality, from Henry Miller and Pablo Picasso to Khalil Gibran and Vladimir Ilyich Lenin. It was a particular favorite of the Spanish and Catalan communities. During the 1920s, Spanish philosopher Miguel de Unamuno convened a daily forum, attended by the likes of Luis Buñuel and Ismael de la Serna.

Cross to the island in the middle of boulevard Raspail on the downhill side.

2 Auguste Rodin's statue of novelist Honoré de Balzac has stood here since 1939. Rodin completed a plaster version in 1891, but the commissioning body, the Société des Gens de Lettres, refused to accept it, claiming that the figure under the cloak didn't look human. It wasn't cast in bronze until 22 years after Rodin's death, and was immediately acknowledged as one of his greatest works and a milestone in modern sculpture.

Sartre and Beauvoir

Return to boulevard du Montparnasse and continue walking west.

3 At 99, boulevard du Montparnasse, on the corner of rue Vavin, is Café Select. Opened in 1925 (by a family named Select), it was the first of the great cafés to remain open all night, and became popular with what Hemingway called "ladies of both sexes."

Henry Miller

In 1929, poet Hart Crane spent six days in jail after a drunken fight with waiters over the bill. The café also was a favorite of writer Henry Miller, filmmaker Luis Buñuel, and of political radical Emma Goldman. James Baldwin wrote most of his novel *Giovanni's Room* here.

James Baldwin

Cross boulevard du Montparnasse.

La Coupole

KIKI
DE MONTPARNASSE
CAFÉ · BOCQUET

Kiki de Montparnasse

4 La Coupole (The Cupola) opened in 1927 at 102, boulevard du Montparnasse, combining a café, restaurant and a basement dance hall with an "American bar" serving the cocktails tourists demanded. Defying André Breton's prohibition on the Surrealists visiting Montparnasse, Louis Aragon was a regular. He met his wife Elsa Triolet here in 1928 and, in 1929, was introduced by Man Ray to Salvador Dalí and Luis Buñuel, who invited him to view their film *Un Chien Andalou,* and decide whether it was truly Surrealist. La Coupole was also patronized by Pablo Picasso, Jean Cocteau's novelist lover Raymond Radiguet, artists Léonard Tsuguharu Foujita, Moise Kisling, Alberto Giacometti and Ossip Zadkine, as well as model Alice Prin, better known as Kiki de Montparnasse.

Originally two stories, the building was rebuilt in 1986, adding offices and apartments above, though the restaurant retains its noisy charm, as well as the original Art Deco floor tiling. The columns are also original, by students of Henri Matisse and Fernand Léger, who had studios on nearby rue Notre-Dame-des-Champs.

Walk back along boulevard du Montparnasse towards boulevard Raspail.

5 On the corner at 108, boulevard du Montparnasse, Le Dôme dates from 1898. In exile before the 1918 revolution, Lenin and Trotsky were regulars, as were Henry Miller, Man Ray and Samuel Beckett. Hemingway's *A Moveable Feast* describes an evening spent with the painter Jules Pascin at the Dôme. The terrace, once open to the street, is now enclosed, and the café itself has become a seafood restaurant.

Make a sharp right turn onto rue Delambre.

6 Japanese painter Léonard Tsuguharu Foujita had his studio at 5, rue Delambre from 1917 until 1926, where he entertained Amedeo Modigliani, Jules Pascin, Chaim Soutine and Fernand Léger. Among his models was Alice Prin, who had become the model and lover of Man Ray.

7 At No. 8 rue Delambre, Samuel Putnam edited the five issues of the influential "little magazine" *The New Review* between 1930 and 1932; Ezra Pound was associate editor. It published numerous expatriate writers, including Henry Miller, Samuel Beckett and Robert McAlmon.

Foujita in Montparnasse

8 From 1926, dancer Isadora Duncan, then in her late 40s, lived at 9, rue Delambre. No longer able to command large sums for her performances, she famously complained: "I don't know where the next bottle of champagne is coming from." She gave private lessons to, among others, her neighbor Foujita. In 1927, she died dramatically in Nice, her neck broken when her scarf caught in the wheel of an automobile.

9 Now the Auberge de Venise, 10, rue Delambre is the site of the former bar Le Dingo (from French slang: *dingue* = crazy). In April 1925, Hemingway and Scott Fitzgerald met here for the first time. Hemingway wrote an introduction to *This Must Be the Place: Memoirs of Montparnasse,* a memoir by its one-time barman, the former boxer Jimmie Charters.

Other clients included Sinclair Lewis, Sherwood Anderson, John Dos Passos, Ezra Pound, Henry Miller and Thornton Wilder.

🔟 11bis, rue Delambre is the former location of the Rosebud Bar, frequented in 1937 by both Jean-Paul Sartre and Simone de Beauvoir, who lived separately in hotels on the street.

🔢 Now the parking garage of the Hôtel Villa Modigliani, 13, rue Delambre was the site of Man Ray's first photography studio after he arrived from New York in July 1921. He lived next door at what was then the Grand Hôtel des Écoles.

🔢 Tristan Tzara, founder of the Dada movement, lived at the Hotel Lenox (formerly Grand Hôtel des Écoles, 15, rue Delambre) in 1921. At the same time, Man Ray occupied Room 32. Henry Miller met Alfred Perlès here in May 1925, and "a friendship was begun which was to color the entire period of my stay in France." The two men later shared an apartment, an episode that inspired Miller's *Quiet Days in Clichy*. Miller also lived here with his wife June from 1928 to 1930.

🔢 Simone de Beauvoir lived at the Hôtel des Bains (33, rue Dealmbre) in 1937.

🔢 Painter Paul Gauguin lived at 35, rue Delambre in the Hôtel Delambre, formerly the Hôtel des Écoles (not to be confused with the *Grand* Hôtel des Écoles at No. 15) in 1891. André Breton, founder of Surrealism, stayed here from 1920 to 1921 after giving up his medical studies. Disliking the triviality of Montparnasse, he moved to less pretentious Montmartre. In 1927, the hotel was home to the young painter Francis Bacon.

Enter boulevard Edgar Quinet, which runs along the side of the Montparnasse Cemetery.

Then & Now

Le Dôme

La Rotonde

Group portrait of American and European artists and performers in Paris: Man Ray, Mina Loy, Tristan Tzara, Jean Cocteau, Ezra Pound, Jane Heap, Kiki de Montparnasse c. 1920s

Sartre and Beauvoir

Man Ray

15 The brothel Le Sphinx was once located here at 31, boulevard Edgar Quinet. Opened in 1931, Le Sphinx was the most lavish of Paris's so-called *maisons de tolerance* (indicating that it operated with the approval of the authorities). Guests at the opening included the mayor of Montparnasse and his wife. The Egyptian décor set new standards in opulence. It was also the first building in Paris to be air-conditioned. Henry Miller wrote the text for its promotional brochures, and took payment "in trade," plus a bonus for each new client introduced. Novelist Lawrence Durrell recalled spending "fabulous hours with Henry Miller at the Sphinx." Other celebrity visitors included bandleader Duke Ellington. Like all France's brothels, Le Sphinx was shut down in 1946 as part of a morality drive spearheaded by Marthe Richard, famous as a spy during World War I and herself a former prostitute.

16 The 1920s lesbian club The Monocle occupied the basement of the building at 14, boulevard Edgar Quinet. It admitted only women, who had to dress in male evening clothes.

Cross to Montparnasse Cemetery.

17 Created from farmland in 1824, this is the resting place of numerous figures from literature, politics and the arts, including the shared grave of Jean-Paul Sartre and Simone de Beauvoir, the plain black marble slab of Samuel Beckett, Man Ray's monument with its reticent epitaph, "Unconcerned, but not Indifferent," and the photograph-decorated grave of singer Serge Gainsbourg.

Signs at the main entrances indicate the general position of most famous graves, but you may need to ask one of the attendants for specific directions.

Exit the cemetery onto boulevard Edgar Quinet and continue towards boulevard Raspail.

18 Film director Luis Buñuel lived at the Hôtel L'Aiglon (232, boulevard Raspail at the corner of boulevard Edgar Quinet) in the 1960s, during the making of *Diary of a Chambermaid, Belle de Jour* and *The Milky Way*. His windows gave a view of the cemetery, which he claimed to find consoling, but which spooked actresses he invited there, in particular Catherine Deneuve. In June 1961, after terrorists bombed the apartment on rue Bonaparte that he shared with his mother, Jean-Paul Sartre moved to Montparnasse, and installed his mother next door to Buñuel.

Cross boulevard Raspail, turn right, then left onto rue Campagne-Première.

Many artists of the late 19th and early 20th centuries lived on this street, which was convenient to the studios on the other side of boulevard du Montparnasse, notably on rue Notre-Dame-des-Champs.

19 In 1926, Man Ray moved into the distinctive building at 31 bis, rue Campagne-Première, designed by André Arfvidson in 1911 and featuring striking ceramics by Alexandre Bigot. It became Ray's primary apartment and studio, though he kept another studio on rue Val-de-Grâce. He lived here with Alice Prin until 1929, and thereafter for three years with Lee Miller, with whom he developed the Rayograph process.

20 Francis Picabia, Marcel Duchamp, Moise Kisling, Man Ray and Kiki de Montparnasse were among the artists who patronised the modest Hôtel

Istria at 29, rue Campagne-Première. A plaque prominently placed on the façade lists a number of them.

21 The Passage d'Enfer (Hell's Passage) is a short lane that makes an abrupt right-hand turn to rejoin boulevard Raspail. In 1871, Arthur Rimbaud lived in a room here, paid for by his lover Paul Verlaine. The Passage reveals some unusual features of Arfvidson's architecture for No. 31 bis, including ventilated serveries designed to keep food cool in that pre-refrigerator era.

22 Formerly the home and studio of pioneering photographer Eugène Atget, 17 bis, rue Campagne-Première became famous after 1927 as the site of Stanley Hayter's printmaking studio Atelier 17. Joan Miró, Salvador Dalí, Alberto Giacometti, Max Ernst, Pablo Picasso, Jacques Lipschitz and Jackson Pollock learned the principles of etching and lithography here.

Eugène Atgent

23 After the Universal Exposition of 1889, some materials were salvaged to create a Cité des Artistes of 100 tiny studios at 9, rue Campagne-Première. Among those who occupied them were Amedeo Modigliani, James McNeill Whistler and Giorgio de Chirico.

Artists working at the Cité des Artistes habitually ate at Chez Rosalie, a modest restaurant founded at 3, rue Campagne Première by retired model Rosalie Tobia. (The building has since been demolished.)

24 On the west corner of rue Campagne Première and boulevard du Montparnasse was the original club Le Jockey. "Go at 11 o'clock," advised a contemporary guide book. "See famous painters and the real Bon Vivants of Paris. An indescribable atmosphere. A sign, reading: 'The only client we ever lost, died'. Low, cracked ceilings and the tattered walls covered with posters. Cartoons painted with shoe polish."

Turn right on boulevard du Montparnasse and cross.

▣ The Closerie des Lilas (The Garden of Lilacs) is the last and most famous of the great Montparnasse cafés, located at 171, boulevard du Montparnasse (corner of boulevard du Montparnasse and boulevard Saint-Michel). Opened in 1847, it was originally a stop on the main coach route out of Paris. During the early 20th century it became a favorite of the Montparnos. Émile Zola dined here with Paul Cézanne. Modigliani, Rimbaud, Apollinaire, Breton, Aragon, Picasso, Sartre, Gide, Eluard, Wilde, Beckett and Man Ray were all regulars.

Closerie des Lilas c. 1920

In 1922, the Dadaists put André Breton "on trial" here for attacking founder Tristan Tzara. Those who sided with Breton became the Surrealists. The café was Hemingway's favorite workplace. He wrote *Big Two-Hearted River* and *Soldier's Home* over *café crèmes* in the calm of its hedge-enclosed terrace; he even set parts of *The Sun Also Rises* at the Closerie. Since then, the café has gone up-market, dividing into an expensive restaurant and a more modest piano bar, the tables of which carry brass plates with the names (occasionally misspelled) of distinguished patrons from former times.

Closerie des Lilas, detail by Charles Vernier

The Port-Royal station opposite the Closerie des Lilas is served by the ⓇⒺⓇ Ⓑ or above-ground railway. To return to central Paris, take one of the many buses that run down boulevard Saint-Michel.

EIFFEL TOWER, NAPOLEON'S TOMB & RODIN MUSEUM

1 Palais de Chaillot
2 Trocadéro Gardens
3 Eiffel Tower
4 Peace Memorial
5 École Militaire
6 Hôtel des Invalides
7 Musée Rodin

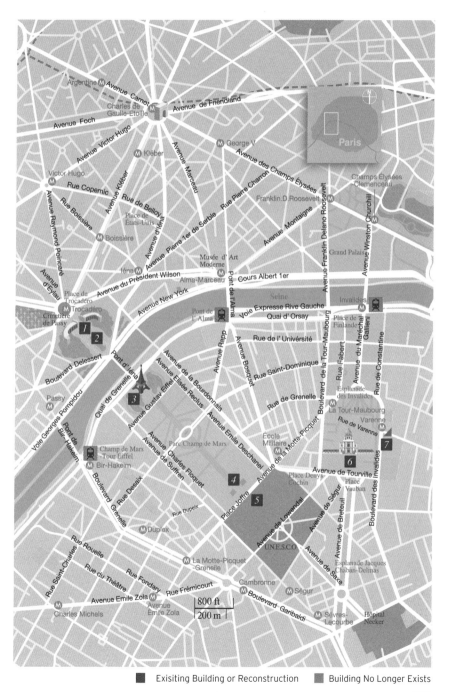

Exisiting Building or Reconstruction   Building No Longer Exists

START:
Métro at Trocadéro

MÉTRO:
Ⓖ or Ⓨ

END:
Métro at Varenne

MÉTRO:
⑬

Eiffel Tower, 1900

Unlike the monuments of pre-Revolution Paris, those of the 19th and 20th centuries tend to be sited on open ground and built for dramatic effect. Napoleon liked a vista, and the builders of the Eiffel Tower learned his lesson. For the walker, this means longer distances between locations, though the resulting views are well worth it.

Exit Métro at Trocadéro (Lines Ⓖ and Ⓨ). Cross place du Trocadéro to Palais de Chaillot.

1 The Palais de Chaillot was designed for the 1937 Exposition Internationale des Arts et Techniques dans la Vie Moderne. A classic of late Art Deco, the complex originally housed the national film museum, the Cinémathèque Française; the museum of anthropology, the Musée de l'Homme; and the Théâtre National Populaire. Today, the building is occupied by the Musée de la Marine, devoted to France's maritime history, and the Cité de l'Architecture, celebrating the monuments of

Adolf Hitler in Paris

France. The anthropological museum, Musée de l'Homme, remains in place, though many former exhibits now reside in the Musée du Quai Branly. The basement (accessed from the Trocadéro Gardens) contains an aquarium, cinemas and a restaurant.

The paved Esplanade between the two wings of the Palais de Chaillot offers the ultimate view of the Eiffel Tower—Adolf Hitler chose it to survey a conquered Paris. Statues of an elephant and a rhinoceros that originally stood here now decorate the forecourt of the Musée d'Orsay.

2 Decend the Esplanade of the Palais de Chaillot to reach the grounds of the Jardin du Trocadéro or Trocadéro Gardens. These gardens feature numerous fountains and art deco statues, in particular Paul Jouve's gilded bronze *Taureau et Daim* (*Bull and Deer*), Georges Guyot's *Chevaux et Chien* (*Horses and Dog*), and Henri Bouchard's 21-foot-high *Apollo*. On the lowest level, next to the Varsovie (or Warsaw) Fountain, a play area for children includes a carousel.

3 Cross the Pont d'Iéna to reach the Eiffel Tower, located on the Champ de Mars. Since 1889, 200 million people have visited the tower. It has 704 steps, but most people prefer the elevators. Though these service its three levels, many visitors don't go higher than the second-story observation deck. The summit of the tower houses Gustave Eiffel's restored office. The many eateries in the tower include the chic Jules Verne Restaurant, named for the author of *20,000 Leagues Under the Sea*. At night, a web of halogen lamps covering the exterior flashes for five minutes at the top of each hour. The Eiffel Tower is open every day year-round, usually between 9:30 a.m. and 11 p.m., with extended hours in the summer. Tickets are required. Expect long waits both for tickets and elevators, particularly in warm weather. You can shorten the delay by purchasing tickets online in advance.
www.eiffel-tower.com

Continue through Parc Champ de Mars to avenue de la Motte-Picquet. The Champ de Mars (The Field of Mars) was originally a military parade ground for the École Militaire.

4 Created in 2000, the Wall of Peace contains the word "Peace" in 32 languages.

5 Designed by Ange-Jacques Gabriel in 1752, the École Militaire was founded to train the sons of poor families. In 1785, Napoleon Bonaparte completed the two-year course in just one year. Now the École de Guerre or School of War, it is a college of advanced military study for members of the armed forces and police.

A statue of Marshal Joseph Joffre stands in front of the École Militaire. In 1914, Joffre was decisive in halting the German advance at the Marne River, a battle so close to Paris that taxis were used to ferry reinforcements to the front.

6 Cross place École Militaire and continue on avenue de Tourville to reach the Hôtel des Invalides (Home for Invalid Soldiers). With its gilded dome and striking location on a park sweeping down to the Seine, the Invalides is one of the glories of Paris. Louis XIV commissioned the military hospital in 1670 and it still functions as a veteran treatment center; today the complex also contains two churches, the Military Museum and the tomb of Napoleon Bonaparte.

Completed in 1735, the Chapelle Saint-Louis des Invalides was originally called the Soldiers' Church and served veterans living in the Invalides, all of whom were required to attend daily mass. It was ransacked during the Revolution, and most of its treasures were taken. The surviving features include the organ casing by Germaine Pilon, completed in 1687. The military banners, many of which originally hung in Notre-Dame, are all that survive after the governor of the Invalides burned most of them in 1814, fearing they would fall into the hands of the allied armies surrounding the city following the fall of Napoleon.

Louis XIV

Église du Dôme

Louis XIV commissioned the towering, 351-foot-high Église du Dôme for the exclusive use of the royal family, allowing them to hear mass at the same time as the commoners in the adjacent Chapel of Saint-Louis, now separated by a glass wall. In 1840, Louis-Philippe retrieved the remains of Napoleon from St. Helena, and commissioned Louis-Tullius-Joachim Visconti to adapt the church as a tomb. His ashes were interred there in 1861. Coffins of tin,

Napoleon, detail, by Ingres at the Musée de l'Armée

277

Funeral ceremony for the transfer of the ashes of the Emperor Napoleon, 1840

Napoleon's coffin

Charles de Gaulle exhibition

lead, oak, mahogany and ebony—one laid within the next—are enclosed in a sarcophagus of Russian red porphyry, resting on a base of green Vosges granite. The emperor's brothers, Jérôme and Joseph, and his son are also buried here. The adjacent crypt became the traditional resting place of French military heroes, including Marshal Ferdinand Foch, the military commander who accepted the German surrender as supreme commander of the Allied armies at the end of World War I. Foch's monument features a life-sized statue of a group of soldiers carrying his coffin.

The Musée de l'Armée, or military museum of the Army of France, occupies several floors of the main building at the Les Invalides. Exhibits include lavishly decorated royal arms and armor, artillery of many centuries, and one of the taxis that carried soldiers to the front in 1914. Three floors are devoted to World War II alone, while an ambitious multi-media exhibition that traces the life and achievements of General and President Charles de Gaulle. For more information on Les Invalides visit **www.invalides.org**

Exit the Hôtel Invalides and make a right onto rue de Grenelle. Take a right onto boulevard des Invalides and walk left to rue de Varenne to reach the Musée Rodin.

7 The sculptures of Auguste Rodin (1840-1917) appear to erupt out of the clay or stone, still marked with the impression of his massive hands. Argumentative, seductive and stubborn, he worked for many years in this building, the Hôtel Biron, built between 1728 and 1730 by a wealthy wig-maker and financial speculator. Turned into a religious school for girls, it was acquired by the

state in 1905 and became a popular studio space. Jean Cocteau and Henri Matisse lived here; dancer Isadora Duncan held classes in a garden studio, now demolished. Poet Rainer Maria Rilke recommended it to Rodin, who bequeathed his extensive collection to the nation, including his own work, that of friends like Renoir and van Gogh, and antiquities dating back to Pharaonic Egypt—on the condition that the building become a museum to display it.

As well as showcasing Rodin's creations and collections, the Musée Rodin presents exhibitions of contemporary art. **www.musee-rodin.fr**

Exit Musée Rodin, return to boulevard des Invalides and head right towards Métro Varenne (line **13**).

INDEX

PHOTO CREDITS:

4-5: The ancient city of Paris, c. 1780.
Courtesy of Everett Collection

8: Saint Denis, carrying his own head, startles citizens of Roman Paris after his decapitation. From the collection of John Baxter

10: Basilique St Denis [6 mai 1917, levée de l'oriflamme] : [photographie de presse] / Agence Rol]
Courtesy of Bibliothèque nationale de France

19: [Jardin du cloître des Petits-Augustins. Tombeau d'Héloïse et d'Abélard] : [dessin] / Vauzelle an 1815
Courtesy of Bibliothèque nationale de France

28: Marie Antoinette and her family stroll the ground of the Palace of Versailles. From the collection of John Baxter

29: Marie-Antoinette, à mi-corps, de profil à gauche, dans un ovale tronqué décoré de fleurs de lys et entouré d'une guirlande de roses : [estampe]
Courtesy of Bibliothèque nationale de France

30: Portrait de Marie Antoinette reine de France conduite au supplice, dessiné à la plume par David... : [dessin] / copié sur l'original existant dans la collection Soulavie
Courtesy of Bibliothèque nationale de France

32: Civi optimo J.I. Guillotin : docteur-régent, ancien professeur de la Faculté de médecine de Paris, né à Saintes : [estampe] / J.M. Moreau del. 1785 ; B.L. Prevost sc.
Courtesy of Bibliothèque nationale de France

34: Public Execution by Guillotine, 1880
From the Collection of John Baxter

41: Napoleon
National Photo Company Collection, Prints & Photographs Division, Library of Congress, LC-F81- 2170

47: Vue du château de la Malmaison à S. M. l'Empereur des Français et roi d'Italie Prise du côté de l'Entrée de Paris l'on voit des deux côtés le Parc : [estampe]
Courtesy of Bibliothèque nationale de France

51: La maison de George Sand à Nohant / Cim
Courtesy of Bibliothèque nationale de France

52: La main gauche de Chopin / Aussoleil, Lyon
Courtesy of Bibliothèque nationale de France

54: Notre Dame de Paris par Victor Hugo, 10 cent[ime]s la livraison : [affiche] / [non identifié]
Courtesy of Bibliothèque nationale de France

57: [Notre-Dame de Paris] : [estampe] / [non identifié]
Courtesy of Bibliothèque nationale de France

58: Favras, faisant amende honorable en face de l'église de Notre-Dame à Paris : le 19 février 1790 : [estampe] / Prieur inv. & del. ; Berthault sculp. ;

[eau-forte par Duplessi-Bertaux]
Courtesy of Bibliothèque nationale de France

60: [Frontispice : Marguerite Gautier] La Dame aux camélias par Alexandre Dumas fils.
[Cote : BnF-micr. R 132634]
Courtesy of Bibliothèque nationale de France

62: Marie Duplessis by Édouard Viénot
From the collection of John Baxter

64: Marie Duplessis, inspiration for La Dame aux Camélias, on her deathbed. From the collection of John Baxter

83: A Communist barricade Cabinet of American Illustration, Prints & Photographs Division, Library of Congress, LC-USZ62-46318

87: Master chef Georges Auguste Escoffier (1846 - 1935). From the collection of John Baxter

96: Courtesans in a private box at the Opéra Garnier. From the collection of John Baxter

98: M. Eiffel, our artist's latest tour de force, June 29, 1889] / Linley Sambourne, [...] del., Paris, June 18, '89. Tissandier Collection, Prints & Photographs Division, Library of Congress, LOT 13401, no. 12

100: Gustave Eiffel, 1888
From the collection of John Baxter

102: G. Eiffel and four other people at the summit of the Eiffel Tower Tissandier Collection, Prints & Photographs Division, Library of Congress, LOT 6001

112: Paris, société rustique à Montmartre : [photographie de presse] / Agence Meurisse
Courtesy of Bibliothèque nationale de France

Bal-musette Montmartre, Théophile Steinlen
From the collection of John Baxter

114: Montmartre pittoresque : Le cabaret du Lapin Agile : [photographie de presse] / Agence Meurisse, 1912
Courtesy of Bibliothèque nationale de France

130: First Division, A.E.F. American Expeditionary Forces. General Pershing Harris & Ewing Collection, Prints & Photographs Division, Library of Congress, LC-H261- 30906

132: First Division, A.E.F. American Expeditionary Forces. General Pershing Leading Parade Harris & Ewing Collection, Prints & Photographs Division, Library of Congress, LC-H261- 30911

133: WWI magazines La Baïonnette and Regiment
From the collection of John Baxter

134: Le général Pershing sur la tombe de Lafayette [cimetière de Picpus à Paris, 13 juin 1917] : [photographie de presse] / [Agence Rol]
Courtesy of Bibliothèque nationale de France

138: UN CHIEN ANDALOU, (aka AN ANDALUSIAN DOG), Simone Mareuil (second row from bottom left), Pierre Bachefft (4th row from bottom right), 1929
Courtesy of Everett Collection

142: Portrait of Man Ray and Salvador Dali, Paris Van Vechten Collection, Prints & Photographs Division, Library of Congress, LOT 12735, no. 968

Dali automicus, Salvador Dali, c. 1948
PH Filing Series Photographs, Prints & Photographs Division, Library of Congress, PH - Halsman (P.), no. 14 (AA size)

144: Gabrielle Bonheur 'Coco' Chanel, 1910
Courtesy of Everett Collection

147: Couturier Coco Chanel with Surrealist artist Salvador Dalí
From the collection of John Baxter

150: Ernest Hemingway's 1923 passport (detail).
Ernest Hemingway Collection, John F. Kennedy Presidential Library and Museum, Boston.

152: Pamplona, Spain, summer 1926. L-R (at table): Gerald Murphy, Sara Murphy, Pauline Pfeiffer, Ernest Hemingway and Hadley Hemingway. Photograph in the Ernest Hemingway Photograph Collection, John F. Kennedy Presidential Library and Museum, Boston.

153: Ernest Hemingway with Sylvia Beach and her staff in front of Shakespeare and Company
From the collection of John Baxter

154: John "Bumby" Hemingway and Gertrude Stein. Paris, 1924. Photograph in the Ernest Hemingway Photograph Collection, John F. Kennedy Presidential Library and Museum, Boston.

155: For Whom the Bell Tolls
From the collection of John Baxter

156: Ernest Hemingway outside of his residence at 13 rue Notre-Dame-des-Champs, Paris, ca. 1924. Photograph in the Ernest Hemingway Photograph Collection, John F. Kennedy Presidential Library and Museum, Boston.

164: Sheet music for Josephine Baker's theme come, showing her in costume with her pet cheetah, Chiquita
From the collection of John Baxter

166: Nora
From the collection of John Baxter

167: Josephine Baker in her famous Banana Skirt
From the collection of John Baxter

172: Young Resistants from Huelgoat in Brittany
From the collection of John Baxter

176: Peter Orlovsky and Allen Ginsberg in Rue St. Andre-des-Arts, December 1956. At that time, they were living in Room 25 of the Beat Hotel.
Photographer: Harold Chapman ©2000 Credit:Topham Picturepoint

179: William Burroughs,outside the Beat Hotel. 1958.
Photographer: Harold Chapman ©2000 Credit:Topham Picturepoint

182: BREATHLESS, (aka A BOUT DE SOUFFLE), from poster art, from left: Jean-Paul Belmondo, Jean Seberg, 1960
Courtesy of Everett Collection

185: FAHRENHEIT 451, director Francois Truffaut, on set, 1966
Courtesy of Everett Collection

187: Cinémathèque Française

© Stéphane Dabrowski / Cf.

190: Jean-Louis Barrault addressing students occupying the Théâtre de l'Odéon in 1968
From the collection of John Baxter

192: 1968 Poster "La Beauté est dans la rue"
From the collection of John Baxter

198: [Galerie et jardins du Palais-Royal] : [dessin]
Courtesy of Bibliothèque nationale de France

199: [Le nº 113. Palais-Royal. 1815. La sortie du nº 113] : [dessin] / Opiz inv. et del.
Courtesy of Bibliothèque nationale de France

201: [Escalier au 13 de la Galerie Vivienne] : [Mai 1906] / Eugène Atget, photogr.
Courtesy of Bibliothèque nationale de France

203: [Le quartier Vivienne] / Eugène Atget, photogr.
Courtesy of Bibliothèque nationale de France

[La Bibliothèque nationale] / Eugène Atget, photogr.
Courtesy of Bibliothèque nationale de France

205: Grand Opera, the largest theatre in the world, cost six million dollars, Paris, France / photographed and published by B.W. Kilburn. Stereograph Cards, Prints & Photographs Division, Library of Congress, STEREO FOREIGN GEOG FILE - France--Paris--Opera

The Opera House, the inauguration of the opera, Paris, France Photochrom Prints, Prints & Photographs Division, Library of Congress, LOT 13418, no. 275

206: Opera model
From the collection of John Baxter

210: Métiers, boutiques et étalages de Paris. [1898-1911] / Eugène Atget, photogr.
Courtesy of Bibliothèque nationale de France

[Le dix-huitième arrondissement de Paris] / Eugène Atget, photogr.
Courtesy of Bibliothèque nationale de France

212: Cabaret du Néant c. 1892
From the collection of John Baxter

Cabaret L'Enfer c. 1899
From the collection of John Baxter

213: [Le neuvième arrondissement de Paris] / Eugène Atget, photogr.
Courtesy of Bibliothèque nationale de France

Métiers, boutiques et étalages de Paris. [1898-1911] / Eugène Atget, photogr.
Courtesy of Bibliothèque nationale de France

215: Frédéric Chopin / d'après un dessin de George Sand, 1870
Courtesy of Bibliothèque nationale de France

217: View from Galeries Lafayette
Courtesy of Everett Collection

220: Moulin de la Galette c. 1840.
From the collection of John Baxter

Moulin de la Galette. Restaurant. Salons. Cabinets. Jardin des Jeux... : [affiche] / [J. Jonchère], 1880
Courtesy of Bibliothèque nationale de France

ABOUT MUSEYON

Named after the Museion, the ancient Egyptian institute dedicated to the muses, Museyon Guides is an independent publisher that explores the world through the lens of cultural obsessions. Intended for frequent fliers and armchair travelers alike, our books are expert-curated and carefully researched, offering rich visuals, practical tips and quality information.

Pick one up and follow your interests...wherever they might go.
For more information vist www.museyon.com

Publisher: Akira Chiba
Editor-in-Chief: Heather Corcoran
Art Director: Ray Yuen
Cover Design: José Antonio Contreras
Maps & Illustration Design: EPI Design Network, Inc.
Copy Editors: Janice Battiste, Cotton Delo, Carrie Funk

Museyon Guides has made every effort to verify that all information included in this guide is accurate and current as of our press date. All details are subject to change.

ABOUT THE AUTHOR

John Baxter is a biographer, film critic, novelist and
broadcaster. Since relocating in Paris in 1989, he
has also written a series of best-selling memoirs and
books about the city, including *We'll Always Have
Paris*, *Cooking for Claudine* and *The Most Beautiful
Walk in the World*. His books on the cinema include
highly praised biographies of Federico Fellini,
Steven Spielberg, Woody Allen, Stanley Kubrick and
Robert DeNiro.